Young, Gifted and Doing It
52 Power Moves for Teens

By: Cassandra Mack

Authors Choice Press

New York Lincoln Shanghai

Young, Gifted and Doing It
52 Power Moves for Teens

Authors Choice Press
an imprint of iUniverse, Inc.

iUniverse books may be ordered through booksellers or by contacting:

iUniverse
2021 Pine Lake Road, Suite 100
Lincoln, NE 68512
www.iuniverse.com
1-800-Authors (1-800-288-4677)

Originally published by Strategies For Empowered Living, Inc.

Because of the dynamic nature of the Internet, any Web addresses or links contained in this book may have changed since publication and may no longer be valid.

The views expressed in this work are solely those of the author and do not necessarily reflect the views of the publisher, and the publisher hereby disclaims any responsibility for them.

ISBN: 978-0-595-46789-1

Printed in the United States of America

Contents

A Message To Teens From The Author

Being a teenager during today's times is filled with many choices and challenges. You are at a critical point in your life in that the decisions you make today can have long term and even lifetime consequences. There's no question that the pressure's on. But despite the challenges that lie ahead of you, you can make it. Believe it or not, there are thousands of teenagers just like you who are on the right track taking positive charge of their lives. Despite what some people think or what the media tries to make you believe, you are not destined to become a statistic for the six o'clock news. You were genetically coded for greatness. You can do and be anything that you set your mind to. If you make the decision to stay on the right track and work towards your goals, you will be a success. Why? Because the most important factor in your success is your determination to succeed. This book was written to serve as your success guide. It will motivate, inspire and challenge you to do what you need to do to become successful in every area of your life – school, work, family, friends and the pursuit of your dreams.

Young, Gifted and Doing It provides you with fifty-two power moves that you can make each week in order to: get your self-esteem into high gear, get along better with your parents, choose friends wisely, go after your goals, develop smart money management habits, make good decisions, take control of the things that can get in the way of your success and develop your full potential. Each power move focuses on a different topic. It should take you about 15 minutes or so to grasp what you need in order to successfully manage that specific issue. By the time you complete this book, you'll not only be better prepared to handle the many issues that confront today's teens, you'll also be able to plan your next power move or moves.

Young, Gifted and Doing It is set up so that you can make one power move per week. That's all it takes – a time commitment of one day per week. And believe it or not, one power move per week can make a big difference, if you are serious about your success.

Although this book is set up for you to use on a weekly basis, you don't have to use it this way. You can look through the table of contents, select the power moves that most interest you and work on those first.

Read the power moves, apply the power moves and share them with your friends. It is my hope that *Young, Gifted and Doing It* will inspire you to go after your dreams and walk in the fullness of your potential.

After you've read and implemented the power moves in this book and have had some success in either achieving one of your goals or overcoming a very difficult obstacle, drop me a note by e-mailing me at: teenpowermove@aol.com I can't wait to hear your success story!

See You On the Path,
Cassandra Mack

A Message From The Author To Parents, Teachers and Youth Service Providers

As you already know, positioning teenagers for success is both challenging and rewarding. One minute it seems like you're getting through, expanding their horizons and helping them make choices that lead to positive outcomes. The next minute, they're resisting your efforts and literally tuning you out. As soon as you begin to make some real headway, it seems like all your efforts are for naught. Just keep planting seeds, because sooner or later they will take root. And your teens will thank you for it – most of the time.

The good news is most teenagers want to succeed. And believe it or not, they want our input and guidance. Most teenagers want to do well in school and make the people who care about them proud. Most teenagers want to go on to college or find a decent paying job where they can build on their strengths, earn the respect of their colleagues and increase their opportunities for growth and advancement. Some want to start their own businesses. They want to stay out of trouble and become productive citizens who vote, advocate for themselves and make a difference in the lives of others. They want to share their knowledge and experiences as well as learn from yours. Most importantly, they want you to see how valuable, capable, smart and competent they are. And it goes without saying that they want to be loved. But they need our help.

Whether you're a parent, an educator, counselor, social worker or an adult who is simply committed to the success of teens, it is important that you help teens to arm themselves with tools and information that will enable them to boost their self-esteem, succeed in school, resist negative peer pressure, rise above adversity and go after their goals with persistent tenacity.

Young, Gifted and Doing It provides teenagers with a blueprint for success in these areas and many more. From taking responsibility for their future, to developing effective time management and study habits, to building high moral character, to developing social skills that they can utilize for the rest of their lives, throughout this book teens are equipped with power moves that they can apply in just about every facet of life.

I truly encourage you to read *Young, Gifted and Doing It* in its entirety including the tips for parents, teachers and youth workers. Then, consider applying one or more of the power moves to your own life and see what a difference it makes. Also, use the discussion guide in the back of this book to explore some of the issues that impact today's teens.

After you have read the book and utilized some of the power moves with your teens, email me at: teenpowermove@aol.com to let me know how things went. Please be sure to write, *"Young, Gifted and Doing It,"* in the subject section of your e-mail. I look forward to hearing from you.

Inspire Success Wherever You're Planted,
Cassandra Mack

Power Move #1
Become the Director and Producer of Your Life

I believe that we are all the directors and producers of our own lives. We decide whether our lives will be a hit or a miss. And when you are the director and producer of your life, anything is possible. As the director, your role is to decide how you want your story to play out. Will it be a melodrama, a horror flick, a comedy, a tragedy or an action-adventure? As the producer, your role is to find the people and resources to help you move your story in the direction that you want it to go in. You are also the star of your story. And as the star, you have two roles: to take charge of your script and to let your light shine brightly by using all of your creative thinking, skills and talents.

There is a wonderful world full of possibilities just waiting for you to let your light shine, but it's up to you to make it happen. You were born with everything that you need to succeed, but you've got to believe this for yourself and act on your beliefs with conviction. It doesn't matter where you come from or what you've been through, it's about where you are going. And the fact that you have made the decision to take steps towards building a positive future strongly suggests that you're already on the right track.

As the director, producer and star of your life, it's important for you to understand that success only happens to those who make it happen. It happens by taking gradual steps towards your goals and being persistent, even when you're faced with obstacles. Believe that you can make it – and you will. Today, make the decision to take charge of your script.

Know-Dream-Believe
Know that you are destined for great things.
Dream big and expect your dreams to come true.
Believe that you can do, be and have anything you set
your heart and mind to. Then, act on your beliefs.

Power Move #2
Keep Your Head Up

On your journey to do better and become better, you are going to be faced with obstacles. Some of these obstacles will come in the form of difficult experiences – like a situation that doesn't work out the way you hoped or being head over heels about someone who doesn't even know your name. Some obstacles will show up as friends – friends who betray you, friends who lead you to danger and friends who never really accepted you in the first place. Then there are some obstacles that will come through your family – like growing up in a chaotic household or not having your parents there for you in the way that you need them to be. And sometimes when obstacles get the best of you, they can make you believe that you are not strong enough to come through it. But you are and you will, if you keep your head up.

On your journey to learn more, do more and have more, you are going to meet many, different kinds of people. Some people will support and encourage you. Others will go out of their way to drag you down. Then there are those who will pretend to like you, but will throw daggers at you behind your back. But don't sweat the haters, because you have too much going for you to let other people take you off your path. The good thing about obstacles is, they make you think on your feet. They prepare you for success. Think about all the successful people in our society. They've all had challenges to overcome. Oprah Winfrey was abused as a child. Les Brown was diagnosed with a learning disorder and today he's one of the top motivational speakers in the country. Albert Einstein did not speak until he was four and did not read until he was nine. So if you've been through or you're going through tough times, you're in good company.

On your journey to the top there will be people who will talk about you, make fun of you, betray you and hurt you deeply. Don't worry about it; you are stronger than you know. You can pray, tune them out, stay out of their way, reach out for support and keep on keeping on.

People can call you names, treat you unkindly and spread rumors about you, but they cannot stop you from becoming all that you were meant to be. Life can deal you a tough hand and throw some harsh situations your way, but it cannot break your spirit or rob you of your destiny as long as you keep your head up.

No matter what you are going through or what you are being challenged with, keep your head up. And when that becomes too difficult to do, be still and know that God is working things out on your behalf.

Power Move #3
Believe In Yourself

I once heard a story of a young woman named Samantha who was tricked into believing in herself. Samantha was a young woman who was poor, grew up in different foster care homes and she suffered from low self-esteem. Samantha lived in a group home where the other girls made fun of her and the staff treated her unkindly. One day on her way to school, she met a fortuneteller who convinced her to give up her monthly stipend for a palm reading. The fortuneteller told Samantha that she was destined to be a successful woman, but in order to live out her destiny she must come back once a week for a palm reading.

Every week Samantha went back to see the fortuneteller. In exchange for a portion of Samantha's stipend, the fortuneteller gave Samantha a piece of advice. Samantha believed the fortuneteller and started taking on the characteristics of a successful young woman. She went on to college and became an assistant manager for a hot, trendy restaurant. She was poised and confident. Samantha became so successful that the girls in the group home could hardly believe that this was the same shy girl who used to walk around with her head down.

One day, by accident, Samantha found out that the fortuneteller was a fraud and that she told the same story to several other young women in the area. At first, Samantha was heartbroken, but because she had adopted successful habits and developed a strong sense of self-confidence, it didn't matter that the fortuneteller was a fake.

She learned a simple life lesson *"If you believe in yourself and act on your beliefs, there's no stopping you."*

Unfortunately, many people go through life feeling like they're not good enough, smart enough or capable enough to make it. And whatever we believe about ourselves becomes true for us, because we always act in accordance with our beliefs. When Samantha did not believe in herself, she lived a frustrated life, but when Samantha began to believe in herself and acted on her beliefs, she lived a successful life. By changing her beliefs about herself, Samantha changed her life for the better. When you believe in yourself and take positive steps in the right direction, you become a powerhouse of possibility. You will tap your unlimited potential, nurture your unique talents and you will begin to see yourself as the phenomenal person you were meant to be.

How far you go in life and how happy you are depend, to a large extent, on how much you believe in yourself and how forcefully you act on your beliefs. Believe that you are special and capable, and you will move mountains.

Here are some questions to help you uncover your unique gifts and talents. Get a pen and a piece of paper, set aside some quiet time and answer the following questions.

- What makes you uniquely you?

- Do you have a funny laugh, a special way of talking, your own style of dressing, a special skill or talent that others seem to always notice?

- What do you like most about yourself?
  - ➢ Your sense of humor
  - ➢ Your ability to make people laugh
  - ➢ Your ability to listen to others when they need someone to talk to

- What hidden talents do you posses?
  - ➢ Are you good with numbers?
  - ➢ Can you sing, dance, draw, sew, do hair, cook, or write poetry?
  - ➢ Are you the person who others come to when they need sound advice?
  - ➢ What subjects are you good at?

More Things That You Can Do To Believe In Yourself

1. Make a list of ten things that you're most proud of

2. Write down three things that you've learned this year.

3. Say something positive about yourself everyday.

4. Build relationships with positive people who support you and push you to excel.

5. Strengthen your skills. Everyday practice something that you're good at or interested in.

6. In your mind, visualize the type of person you would like to become and take one small step each day to become that person.

Power Move #4
Get In The Driver's Seat

You are capable of determining the outcome of just about every situation you face by getting in the driver's seat of your life. Too often, people escape responsibility by blaming others for the choices they make. While we cannot control everything that happens to us, we can certainly control how we respond. We can also control the day-to-day choices that we make.

Everyday you and I have a choice about how we live our lives. No matter what you've been through or what your current situation is, you are the one who determines how far you go in life. And where you end up in life is entirely up to you. You determine how much education you get, what kind of career you'll have, who you hang out with, how soon you become a parent and how much effort you put into fulfilling your dreams. I once heard that there are three kinds of people: those who play to win, those who sit on the sidelines, and those who play halfway. How are you playing it?

Being in it to win it means getting in the driver's seat and taking responsibility for the direction of your life. It means that you have to stop making excuses for not living up to your full potential and that you move beyond the mindset of powerlessness, because you do have power. Even if you're faced with obstacles, if you stay the course, you can come through any challenge that life sends your way stronger and wiser. In no way am I diminishing the obstacles in your life, because obstacles are real and they can affect your life in unimaginable ways. What I am saying is, if you are serious about making it, then you must work to overcome the obstacles that stand in your way.

Let's look at some ways that you can get in the driver's seat of your life right now.

Develop A Can-Do Mindset

A can-do mindset is a mindset that says, "I can do anything that I set my mind to." It's amazing what you can accomplish with a can-do attitude. A person with a can-do mindset takes the initiative. A can-do person is persistent, focused and creative. A can-do person is determined to make things happen. So let me ask you, are you a can-do person? If not, what will you do to become a can-do?

Keep Your Attitude In Check

Have you ever had a friend who had a jacked-up attitude? You know the type, always on the defensive, has a big chip on his or her shoulder, hardly ever smiles and never speaks unless you speak first. After a while, you get tired of their attitude and you either keep your distance or stop hanging out with them all together. The same thing goes for other people when you give off a negative attitude. This is why it is important that you keep your attitude in check. Be kind to people. And if you're having a bad day, don't take it out on others.

Take The Initiative

Getting in the driver's seat of your life also means taking the initiative and seizing every opportunity that awaits you. Don't wait for the teacher to call on you, raise your hand and show the teacher that you are A-student material. Don't wait for the perfect job to fall in your lap, create it. Get together with a friend and start a babysitting chub, a tutoring service, a dog walking service or any other kind of business that you can dream up.

Make Good Decisions

Everyday you are faced with many important decisions to make. A single decision can have lifelong consequences. Some people think that not making a decision is the easiest thing to do, so they waiver back and forth. These people never become successful, because they cannot make up their minds. At every point in your life there are choices and you'll have to decide what to do and what not to do. Your life is shaped by decisions. Following are seven steps to help you make better decisions.

Seven Steps to Help You Make Better Decisions

1. Identify the problem or decision to be made.

2. List all of your options.

3. Write down the pros and cons for each option.

4. Choose the best option.

5. Put your decision into action.

6. Evaluate your decision. *(Make sure you've made the best decision)*

7. Re-evaluate your situation. *(Make sure you've identified the problem correctly and that the option you've selected is still right for you.)*

Identifying Simple Ways to Take Responsibility

Please list all the ways that you can take responsibility for your life right now. Could you work on your attitude? Improve your grades? Develop better study habits? Look for a part-time job to earn extra money?

_____

_____

_____

_____

_____

_____

_____

_____

Is there anything in your life that you can take responsibility for that you are not?

_____

_____

_____

_____

_____

_____

_____

_____

_____

_____

_____

_____

_____

_____

_____

_____

Write down three things that you can do to become more responsible?

_____

_____

_____

_____

_____

_____

_____

_____

_____

_____

Power Move #5
Don't Hate, Congratulate

When things don't turn out the way we think they should for us, but turn out completely swell for someone else, sometimes we compare our situation with the other person's, and allow petty jealousy to get the best of us. When someone else is more popular, has more material possessions or just seems to have a better life, the typical response is to become envious or jealous.

Envy and jealousy are the cornerstones of misery. Why? Because as long as you are focusing your attention on what another person has or what another person is doing, then you cannot focus your attention on becoming the best person that you can be. The time you spend envying and comparing yourself to other people is time that could be better spent nurturing your talents, setting goals and sharpening your skills. The truth is; it doesn't make any sense to compare yourself to other people, because the only comparison that really counts is the one you make against your own potential.

Every now and then, it's a good idea to look back at your life to see how much you've grown, how far you've come and how much you've got it going on in your own right. A periodic self-review allows you to acknowledge your own successes and take stock of the many attributes that you already posses.

Let's do a quick review. Set aside some quiet time and reflect on all that you've done right and all the ways you've grown over the last year.

_____
_____
_____
_____
_____

- What character traits have you strengthened? Are you more honest with yourself and others? Do you control your temper when you feel like blowing your lid? Are you able to express yourself without becoming explosive or getting an attitude? Are you more organized? Are you studying more?

- Have you been more supportive of others? Are you kinder than you were last year? Do you get along better with your family? Did you help a friend out who was going through a tough time? Did you encourage someone who was feeling down? Did you give up your seat on the bus or subway for an elderly person? Did you help out with a special project or volunteer for a good cause?

- What have you achieved or accomplished over the past year? Did you improve your grades? Did you participate in a leadership program? Did you learn a new skill or hobby? Did you complete an important project?

The answers to these questions will help you to see your own worth and value as a person. They will also help you to see how talented you are and how much you have to offer. This way you'll be able to see for yourself that there is never a good reason to be jealous of anyone else. Why? Because you are unique and wonderful in your own right.

So the next time you are tempted to hate on someone else, think about how blessed and gifted you are and don't hate, just congratulate.

Power Move #6
Drop The Drama

This girl I used to hang out with back in the day put the *QUEEN* in drama queen. Her life was a never-ending saga. And while most of us liked to hear about her roller coaster, escapades, privately we felt that she put herself in risky situations just to satisfy her thirst for melodrama. There's no question that life is filled with drama, especially during the teen years. But it's up to you to decide whether or not to get caught up in it. By making the decision to drop the drama (at least some of it) you'll be more in control of your life.

Of course, dropping the drama is not that easy, because most of us are intrigued by a little melodrama. But when chaos and craziness take over your life, they get in the way of you living up to your full potential. Think about it: if you are constantly caught up in drama, your grades suffer, you are not as focused as you need to be, you get all worked up over things you shouldn't sweat and you get other people involved in your madness. The problem with drama is, it never ends unless you stop feeding it. Getting caught up in drama saps an enormous amount of mental energy and it prevents you from focusing on what really matters.

Dropping the Drama

Here are three questions to help you drop the drama?

- If your life was a day time soap opera what would the title be and why?

- What kind of drama have you had over the past year?

- Write down three or more things that you can do right now to drop some of the drama from your life?

Power Move # 7
In All That You Do Have a Purpose

A story is told of a young man passing through a small town on his way to a big city. Accidentally, he made a wrong turn and ended up off course. After driving several miles trying to find his way back to the main highway, he stopped by a local coffee shop. As the waitress got ready to take his order, he said "I think I'm lost and I need to get back on the main highway." The waitress smiled at the young man and asked, "Do you know where you are?" The young man replied, "I'm not sure, but I know where I'm headed." The waitress finished taking his order and said young man "You're not lost; you just need some basic directions." She then told the young man how to get back on course.

Believe it or not, many people go through life without a real sense of purpose. They have no idea where they want to go in life. If you ask them what they want to do or where they want to end up in life, they look at you with a blank stare. And since they do not have a real sense of purpose, they just aimlessly pass through life feeling lost and misdirected. Many people don't get what they want out of life, not because they don't have the talent or capability, but simply because they do not have a clear sense of purpose.

Your life is like a journey and where you end up is entirely up to you. If you want to make it to your desired destination, then you need to have a clear sense of direction (*your purpose*). Your purpose is not limited to your education or career. It's not what other people say you should do with your life. Your purpose is not defined by your past. Your purpose answers the questions, "Why am I here and what do I want to do, be and have in life?"

Your purpose is not only what you want out of life, but also what you want to contribute to life. And as you grow and become more aware of your needs as well as the needs of the larger community, your purpose will become clearer to you.

Spend some time thinking about what you really want out of life and what direction you want your life to go in. Look at your current situation and think about where you want to end up. When you are ready, take some time out to answer the following questions.

What would you like to do, be and have in life?

_____

_____

_____

What do you feel called or destined to do?

_____

_____

_____

What brings you joy?

_____

_____

_____

Where do you see your life heading?

_____

_____

_____

Who are you? Write down at least fifteen words that describe who you are.

_____

_____

_____

What can you contribute to life that would make you feel special?

_____

_____

_____

What can you contribute to life that would enhance or improve the lives of others?

_____

_____

_____

Are you moving in a direction that will ultimately take you where you want to go?

_____

_____

_____

Answering these questions should help you begin to figure out what your purpose is in life.

Let's take a more detailed look at purpose. I want you to get in the habit of having a purpose for everything you do. This way every step you take will lead you to where you ultimately want to be in life.

Have a Purpose for Your Education

Besides school being something that you have to do, learn to see school as a tool for success. The more education you have, the more options you will have in life.

Have a Purpose for Getting and Keeping a Job

Having a part-time or weekend job is a great way to earn extra money and gain work experience. The more work experience you acquire, the more career choices you'll have.

Have a Purpose for How You Spend Your Free Time

What do you do with your free time? Are you involved in any special activities? Are you part of a team or club? Getting involved in extracurricular activities is a good way to begin to discover your purpose. As you find out about your likes and dislikes and nurture your talents, you'll develop a stronger sense of purpose.

A good way to get clear about your purpose is to write a purpose statement. Your purpose statement should serve as a foundation to guide you on your journey towards success. It is the reason for the journey. Think about the kind of life that you ultimately want to have and let these thoughts be your guide as you write your purpose statement. Here are some examples of purpose statements.

"I intend to help other girls learn that their bodies are temples." Awilda, 16

"My purpose is to help kids in foster care know their rights and grow up to be strong leaders." Charles, 15

I want to create a better life for my daughter. I want her to know that she can do anything she sets her mind to. I know that I have what it takes to make it." Jackie, 17

25

A clear purpose statement takes patience and practice. In order to write a purpose statement that clearly sums up what you ultimately want out of life, you'll probably need to make several attempts at it. That's ok. The most important thing is that you write your purpose statement down. This way you'll always have it handy to keep you on the right track.

My purpose is:

_____

_____

_____

_____

My purpose is:

_____

_____

_____

_____

My Purpose Statement:

_____

_____

_____

_____

Over the next couple of weeks, review your purpose statement and refine it. Make sure that it's clear and concise. Most importantly, make sure that you take your purpose statement seriously. Post your purpose statement where you can review it daily and let your actions be consistent with your purpose.

Power Move #8
Set S.M.A.R.T Goals

One day a guidance counselor at a local high school was assisting a young man who was trying to decide what college to apply for. During the meeting the guidance counselor said, "In order to help you pick the college that's most suited to your needs and goals, I need to know a little bit about what you want to do with your life." The young man looked at the guidance counselor with a blank stare and said "I don't know, I never really thought about it." The counselor replied, "How can you expect me to help you get where you need to go, if you don't have any idea where you are going?"

You may not realize it yet, but having goals is very important. Goals help you move towards your purpose. Goals help you break down your purpose into bite-size action steps. It's even better to write your goals down, because by putting your goals on paper, you'll have a plan in place that will enable you to chart your course of action. Putting your goals on paper says that you are serious about your success.

In order for a goal to be attainable, it must be a S.M.A.R.T goal. S.M.A.R.T goals are goals that are *Small*, *Measurable*, *Achievable*, *Realistic*, and *Time-driven*. Lets say that one of your goals is to improve your academic performance. In order for this to be a S.M.A.R.T goal you must first, take small steps toward your goal such as putting in more hours of study or getting a tutor. Second you must measure your progress. This means, you must come up with a way to figure out how you are going to determine if you're moving closer to your goals. Are you getting more positive feedback from your teachers? Are you participating more in class?

Third, you need to ask yourself, "Is this goal achievable?" The answer should be yes, because we've already established that you are the director and producer of your life and as such you have the power to determine how your story plays out. Fourth, make sure the goal is realistic. And finally, your goal needs to be time-driven, like next semester or next marking period.

Here are 9 keys for setting and achieving your goals:

1. Identify Your Goals
List all the things you want to do, be and have. What kind of person do you want to become? What do you want to accomplish in life? What do you want to have? What kind of lifestyle do you want to live? What do you want to contribute?

2. Describe Your Goals
Describe your ideal life, ideal career, ideal place to live and your ideal kinds of relationships.

3. Take Action Toward Your Goals
What small steps can you take this week, tomorrow, today that will lead you closer to your goals?

4. Identify the Resources You'll Need
What resources will you need to help you reach your goals? Will you need access to a computer? Will you need to get connected to certain people or organizations?

5. Identify the People Who Can Help You
Who are the people you need to build relationships with to help you reach your goals? Is there a family member, special teacher, or a counselor who can offer you encouragement and advice?

6. _Identify the Skills, Habits and Character Traits That You Will Need to Develop_

What skills, habits, or character traits do you need to develop or enhance in order to reach your goals? Do you need to be more focused, more patient, more disciplined? Do you need to keep your attitude in check? Do you need to develop better time management or money management habits?

7. _Figure Out How You Will Measure Your Progress_

How will you know when you're getting closer to your goals? Will you write in a journal? Will you form a goal setting group and check-in with each other regularly to see if you are getting closer you are to your goals?

8. _Set A Time Frame for Each Goal_

After you write down your goals, set a time frame for each goal. Pick two goals from your list and think about when you would like to accomplish each goal – next year, six months from now, next week, tomorrow.

9. _Reward Yourself Each Time You Accomplish A Goal_

Every time you accomplish a goal, even a small one, reward yourself. Put a gold star in your journal, treat yourself to an ice cream cone, rent your favorite movie, write yourself an accomplishment letter.

The keys to setting S.M.A.R.T. goals are to think about what you want out of life and then map out a step-by-step plan to make it happen. Go for your goals. You can do it.

Power Move #9
Watch Your Mouth

Believe it or not, your mouth can be your biggest asset or your greatest liability, depending on how you use it. Whether you are long-winded, loose lipped, smooth as silk or you shoot straight from the hip; what comes out of your mouth is a direct reflection of your character and level of maturity. Your mouth has power. It has the power to build by speaking words of encouragement and it has the power to destroy by speaking hurtful words. This is why it is often said that the tongue is mightier than the sword – because words can kill.

Any person on the path to success knows that it's not only what one does that counts, but also what one says. By managing your mouth, you learn to refrain from saying things that you might later regret. Whenever we speak without thinking about what's coming out of our mouths, we take a risk – the risk of having what we say misunderstood, the risk of betraying someone else's confidence and the risk of saying something that might later get us into trouble.

Managing your mouth not only means being mindful of what you say when you talk to other people, but also being mindful of the things you say to yourself. What do you say when you talk to yourself? Do you say things like? *"I'm ugly." "I'll never make it." I can't do it."* Or, do you say things like? *"I'm good looking." "I'm going to make it." "I can do anything I set my mind to."* What you say to yourself has a tremendous impact on how successful you become. This is why it is so important that you say positive things to yourself.

Managing your mouth also means resisting the urge to gossip. Everyone loves a good story. And most people like to gossip or at least listen to it. Sometimes you may even find yourself gossiping with one of your friends about the other.

And before you know it, you've let a secret slip, fed a rumor or you're being mean just for the heck of it. What you need to know is, every time you dish out or listen to hurtful gossip you are sending a powerful message about yourself. You are saying, *I cannot be trusted to safeguard private information or counted on for emotional support.*

When managing your mouth it's also important to be easy on the swears. In other words, don't use profanity. When you have to use obscene language and curse words to get your point across, what you are really saying is, *I don't have the personal decency or the vocabulary to express myself appropriately.*

So before you open up your mouth, be mindful of the power that you are about to unleash.

Power Move #10
Be Mindful of the Company You Keep

I'm not going to lie to you: when you're a teenager it seems like there's nothing better than hanging out with friends who accept you and make you feel like you're part of the clique. It's ok to want to be accepted by your peers. In fact, it is a normal part of teenage development. But don't let your quest to be accepted by your friends and classmates cause you to hang with people who drag you down.

If you really want to make it in this world, you have to choose your friends wisely. Why? Because your friends play an important role in your life. They can influence your attitude, reputation, the decisions you make, and where you end up in life. It's hard, but there will be times when you are going to have to leave some friends alone. If you have friends who are getting high, not going to school, gang-banging, or doing anything else that could potentially bring you down, then the smartest move you can make is to not hang out with those friends. This does not mean that you can't be cordial by saying hi and bye. What it does mean is that you should limit your conversation to hi and bye, and keep it moving.

Take some time out to think about the people you hang out with. Are they friends or foes? Here are some questions that will help you decide which friends you should keep and which friends you should leave alone.

Write down the names of all the people that you hang out with in the space below. Then go down your list and ask yourself the following questions.

_____

_____

_____

_____

_____

1. Is this person good for me or bad for me?

2. How does this person enhance my life? If this person does not enhance my life, then why am I hanging out with him/her?

3. Where is this friend headed? Is he/she headed for success or is he/she headed for trouble?

4. Does this friend participate in activities that make his/her life better or does this friend participate in activities that make his/her life worse?

5. How does this person treat me? Does this person treat me with respect and kindness or is he/she mean to me?

6. How do I feel about myself when I am around this person? Do I feel supported, encouraged and uplifted or do I feel bad when I'm around this person?

7. Is this person there for me when I need him or her?

8. Do I trust this person to keep my confidence and watch my back?

The answers to these questions will help you to decide whether or not the people you hang out with are friends or foes. If you are serious about making it, then you'll need to be mindful of the company you keep. Think of the eagle the most majestic of all birds. When you watch an eagle fly, you'll notice that they eagle does not fly with chickens or vultures. It flies with other eagles or it flies solo. As you spread your wings, look for other eagles to fly with.

Power Move #11
Don't Let The Past Keep You From Moving Forward

Negative past experiences can affect us for the rest of our lives, if we do not make the choice to make peace with the past. Some people are born into negative circumstances, while others experience negative situations as they move forward in life. No matter what has happened to you, or what other people have done, you cannot let your past prevent you from moving forward. It can be difficult, but it is not impossible.

Far too often, people carry around unresolved feelings of anger, hurt and fear. These feelings can grow inside of you like cancer and will make you look at life through a terminally ill lens. When unresolved feelings take over your emotions and your life, you can get so consumed with being scared, resentful, or wanting to get even, that you leave no room for the good to come in. You can become so accustomed to focusing on the negative, that you will not be able to see blessings and good fortune when they come into your life. There are times when it is difficult to make sense out of our experiences. There are also times when life deals us a bad hand. But every time you choose to live in the past, you stay stuck in the mindset of powerlessness, you have difficulty envisioning a positive life for yourself and it takes you much longer to achieve your goals. Why? Because if you are stuck in the past, chances are, you may not develop the confidence and determination that are necessary for you to rise above adversity in order to grow into your full potential.

Like many people, you may have been through certain situations that might have caused you a lot of pain and suffering. The good news is you don't have to deal with your feelings alone. There are many healthy ways for you to deal with your feelings. For starters, you can talk your feelings through with a responsible adult you trust. You can talk to a counselor or your favorite teacher. You can join a support group. It doesn't matter so much who you reach out to, as long as you reach out for help.

There are many places where you can go for help. I have provided a resource listing for you in the back of this book. So if you don't know where to go, you now have a place to start.

Contrary to what many teens believe, there is nothing wrong with seeking help. Reaching out for help does not mean that you are not normal or that you're crazy. It simply means that you are dealing with a situation that is too heavy for you to bear alone. Believe it or not, reaching out for help when you need it is a sign of strength and courage.

When you feel ready, set aside some quiet time and answer the questions in this section. If it feels too scary to answer them alone, find an adult you trust and go through the questions together.

- Is there any situation that you've been through that makes it difficult for you to move forward?
- Are you holding on to a painful secret that you need to tell someone about?
- Are you carrying around any unresolved feelings of hurt, fear, or anger that you believe are holding you back?
- What caused you to develop these feelings?
- Who could you talk to about these feelings?
- How would you like to feel in the near future?
- What steps can you take to begin to make peace with your experiences and feel more in control of your life?

By answering these questions, you now have information about the feelings that are preventing you from moving forward. Now that you've identified these feelings, you can take the necessary steps to better deal with them. When you deal with your feelings in a healthy way, you'll be able to move forward in life.

It's not what happens to us that defines us. It is what we do with what happens to us that shows how strong and resilient we truly are. You are stronger than your past.

Power Move # 12
Put Your Best Foot Forward

You cannot sit on the side of the pool, stick your toe in the water and say, "I've just finished taking a swim." You have to be willing to get in the water. Otherwise you are not swimming; you're just wading. And if you are going to wade through life, then you might as well swim in the toddler pool. Many people wade through life without ever making the full leap. They put forth 50% effort and wonder why they get back a 50% result.

If you plan on being successful, if you are serious about making it, you've got to give 100%. You will always get out of life what you put into it. Just like putting money in the bank, the more you put in, the more you're able to take out. The more you study, the better your grades become. The harder you work, the more you increase your chances of being promoted. The more you work at a talent or hobby, the better you get at it. It's just that simple. If you put forth the extra effort, you will achieve better results.

I believe that you should never stop trying to do your best, even if you do not get the results that you expect. By putting your best foot forward, you increase your opportunities for successful results. All of us need to put forth our best effort. Putting your best foot forward allows you to grow, push past your fears, learn something new and move beyond your comfort zone.

These self-evaluation questions will help you to figure out whether or not you are putting your best foot forward.

- Are you doing the best you can in school? If not, what steps can you take immediately in order to bring your grades up? If yes, keep up the good work.

- If you have a part-time or weekend job, are you being the best worker that you can be? If not, what steps can you take immediately to become a better employee? If yes, keep up the good work.

- Do you try to get along with your parents? If not, what steps can you take immediately in order to get along better with your parents? If yes, keep up the good work.

- Are you respectful of your teachers and other adults? If not, what steps can you take to become more respectful? If yes, keep up the good work.

- Are there any other areas in your life where you need to put forth a little extra effort? What steps can you take immediately to put forth a little extra effort?

The answer to these questions should help you examine the areas of your life where you could be doing better. Make the commitment to put your best foot forward. It pays.

Power Move #13
Choose Your Battles

In life, you will meet people who will say and do things that will get under your skin, work your last nerve and push you to the tipping point. Usually when this happens, most people lose their cool and retaliate. But most of the time, it's just not worth it. This was the hardest lesson for me to learn because growing up I had a tendency to be tit-for-tat. And there are three things wrong with a tit-for-tat attitude. First, it takes up too much time that could be better spent doing something positive. Second, your life becomes one big battleground with you fighting over things that are really not worth your time and energy. Third, people will begin to distance themselves from you because no one wants to be around someone who always wants to argue and fight.

Sometimes you may feel perfectly justified in letting someone "really have it." But after you've had a moment to calm down and carefully look back at the situation, you may regret your actions. You may think that by arguing your point or going out of your way to prove how right you are, that you come out on top. But the truth is you push people away, because you make it too difficult to get along with you.

Anger is a powerful emotion and when you go into conflict mode over every little issue, you allow that anger to build up like a pot of boiling water waiting to explode. In the end the other person has gotten the best of you. Sometimes you have to just let things go. This does not mean that you should let people walk all over you. It simply means that you'd be better off if you didn't let other people get to you as often. There are better ways to deal with people who say and do things that upset you. When you are calm, you can tell the other person how you feel. You can write your feelings down in a journal.

Before battling it out with someone stop and ask yourself, "What will I gain by blowing my lid?"

By taking a few minutes to collect your thoughts you take control of the situation. And being mature enough to control your emotions enables you to think before you act or react. Many times when people do things that make us angry we react first and think later. We impulsively say or do something to retaliate without thinking about the consequences or how our behavior might jeopardize our relationship with this person. The key to choosing your battles is, to rate the importance of the potential battle. Ask yourself, "Is this situation worth sweating?" Very often the answer will be "no." When you choose your battles rather than allowing your battles to choose you, you will live a healthier and less stressed life.

Power Move #14
Keep a Clear Head

"I think better when I'm high." A little chronic never hurt anyone." "I don't have a problem with alcohol, I just drink every once in a while."

Puh-leeze, any teen with an ounce of common sense who is serious about making it knows that smoking, drinking, and doing drugs of any kind is not cool. It is addictive and destructive. Don't ever let your quest to be down with the crowd or escape life's problems, drive you to do anything that could destroy you. The simple truth is, you cannot escape life's problems by zoning out on drugs. As for peer pressure, real friends would never ask you to do anything that could potentially bring harm to you.

The simple fact is, that mood and mind altering chemicals like marijuana, cocaine, mesc, PCP, and alcohol, not only destroy your body, they impair your judgment causing you to make bad decisions. No one ever thinks that they are going to become addicted, but drinking alcohol and smoking marijuana opens the gate to harder drugs. And once you open up this gate there is no way that you can know for certain that you will not develop an addiction.

Most people who use drugs think that drug addiction is something that happens to other people and that they can quit smoking and drinking anytime they want to. But the truth is, when you use drugs you are no longer in control; the drugs are. When you get the urge to get high, you get high even though you know that drugs will destroy you. You may lie, steal, put yourself in dangerous situations and hurt other people just to get high. You smell bad, your teeth turn yellow and no one who is on the positive track will want to have anything to do with you.

Think about how pitiful it is to have to stand on the corner or in the hallway of an abandoned building getting high, unable to resist the urge. And think about how much it costs to get high. You could spend that extra money on other things such as CD's, movies, clothes, or anything else that you like. Believe me, you are not missing out on anything if you stay away from drugs. You don't need to experiment with anything that could possibly harm or kill you. The short-term high is never worth the long-term harmful effects that follow. Getting high won't make you more popular and it won't make you look cool. It will make you look like a loser.

Power Move #15
Keep It On Lock

In other words, *"Hold off On Sex!"* I know. I know. You really don't want to hear it. You probably saw a few episodes of "Sex And The City" and now you want to be like Samantha the sex kitten. Or, you went out and bought Jay Z's "Big Pimping" CD and now you want to get your swerve on with every girl from Hollis to Hollywood. Or, maybe you're really in love and you think you might be ready to go all the way. Before you call your girls, before you ask your boys for a copy of the Player's Manual, before you make a hasty decision. Just stop and hear me out. The drama you save may be your own.

Before you get your swerve on, think about this:

- The decision to have sex can have consequences that you may have to endure for the rest of your life. Are you willing to take that chance?

- You may become a parent before you are ready. And raising a child while you're still in high school is very difficult.

- You may contract a disease that you cannot get rid of like Herpes or HIV. And when you are taking several medications a day to manage the disease or you have to tell your new boyfriend or girlfriend that you have a sexually transmitted disease, I guarantee you won't be reminiscing about how good your sexual encounters were.

If you are thinking about having sex, the smartest choice for you is to wait. The decision to have sex can affect your health, your education, your goals, how soon you have to give up your freedom to raise a child and so much more. You've got to be sure that you won't have any regrets when it's all said and done. Sex will not make you more popular, because your real friends will accept you whether you are doing it or not. And contrary to popular belief, everyone is not doing it.

Choosing to hold off on sex is not a choice that only a virgin can make. Even if you've had sex in the past, you can choose abstinence.

We are free to choose our paths, but we cannot choose the consequences that come with the paths we take. This is why it's a good idea to hold off on sex while you're in high school. But this is a decision that only you can make. I hope you make the smart choice.

Here are nine things that you can do to focus your attention away from sex. You can:

1. Study hard and get good grades.
2. Get involved in extracurricular activities such as: sports, dance, music, art, poetry and any other activities that channel your creative energy.
3. Discover your fashion sense. You can follow some of the clothing trends, but hook it up with your own personal style.
4. Join a club or start one of your own.
5. Participate in a community service project and make a few friends while doing good for your community.
6. Eat healthy and exercise. You'll look and feel better.
7. Be a role model by mentoring a child.
8. Turn your hobby or something you're really good at into a part-time business.
9. Start an abstinence campaign in your school. (Ex. *"It's cool to be a virgin"* or *"I'm abstaining and I'm proud of it."*)

Power Move #16
Protect Yourself

If I had my way, every teen would abstain and I wouldn't have to offer a power move for those of you who are sexually active. But the reality is some of you are. For those of you who are having sex, what you need to realize is, that you are one of the fastest growing populations contracting HIV and AIDS. You're also the group who has a high number of children out of wedlock that you cannot financially support. I know that a smart teen doesn't want to catch something that they cannot get rid of. I also know you don't want to be raising children or getting caught up in baby mama and baby papa drama, when you could be hanging out and enjoying your teenage years. So protect yourself.

If you are sexually active don't take sex lightly. Casual sex is not cool. Having multiple partners is not cool. It's dangerous. Making love is one of the most intimate experiences that two people can share. It's not just physical. At its best, it is a mental, spiritual, and emotional union between two people who love each other and are committed to one another. It was intended for marriage. So before you make the decision to have sex, you need to think things through and weigh all the pros and cons. You need to think things through carefully and anticipate potential consequences. Because if you wait until things get hot and heavy and get caught up in the heat of the moment, you might make the wrong decision. It just makes good sense to take some time out to think things through before putting yourself in a situation that may have lifetime repercussions.

If despite everything I've said you are dead set on having sex, talk things over with your parents, an older family member or your school counselor. This way you'll have someone with more life experience to provide you with guidance and accurate information.

I know. I know. You're probably thinking "Are you crazy?" "I can't even say the word sex in front of my parents, let alone tell them that I am thinking about doing it." But the bottom line is if you get yourself into a difficult situation, you will need the guidance and support of your parents and other trusted adults to see you through it.

Having sex prematurely can take you off your path and force you to have to make adult decisions and take on adult responsibilities before you are mentally, emotionally and financially ready. And if things don't work out between you and your partner, sex can make your life more complicated than it has to be. It is to your advantage to abstain.

If you do nothing else I've said **please, please, please** protect yourself. You've got too much going for you to cut your life short by contracting HIV or to spend the time you should be spending enjoying you adolescent years, taking care of a child.

Power Move #17
Know Where You Stand

There's an old saying that goes, "If you don't stand for something you will fall for anything." And time and time again this statement has proven itself to be true. Because if you are not clear about what's important to you, then you will not be able to stand by your beliefs when you are faced with difficult decisions.

In order to succeed in this world, you have to know what's important to you. You have to have a clear set of values. Your values are the things that you strongly believe in. Your values determine every decision you make. So when you find that you're having a tough time making or sticking to a decision, it usually means that you are not clear about what you value most in that particular situation. Let's say that your friends are pressuring you to get high and you have a value code that says, "I do not get high." Then saying no to your friends should be pretty easy even if they make fun of you. On the other hand, let's say that you don't know what your values are, then you might be tempted to give into the pressure to try drugs. This is why it is so important that you become real clear about what you value most.

When you know what your values are, decision-making becomes a whole lot easier. Why? Because if you know what's important to you, you'll be comfortable making your own decisions no matter what other people say or do. And further, once you make a good decision you'll be better able to stand by it.

Let's take some time out to clarify your values. To figure out what your values are, ask yourself: "What's most important to me in life?" Is it education? Family? Spirituality? Health? Getting along with my parents? Money? Peace? Happiness? Being a good person? Giving back to the community? Building positive friendships?

Write your values down in their order of importance to you, starting with the most important one and ending with the least.

1) _____

2) _____

3) _____
4) _____
5) _____
6) _____
7) _____
8) _____
9) _____
10) _____

When you are finished, review your values and evaluate whether or not they are helping you to reach your goals or hindering you. If a value is preventing you from reaching your goals, eliminate it and adopt a new value that is more in line with where you want to go in life. As you review your values, you may find that the order of importance changes. What was most important to you a year ago may not be as important now. That's ok. As you grow and develop, your values often change.

Sometimes it can be difficult to get a clear idea of your values, because everyone else is telling you what should be important to you. But only you can decide which values are important to you. Your parents and teachers may guide you, but ultimately you determine your values. Here are some questions that will help you figure out what's important to you.

1. If a good year blimp were to fly across the sky with a banner describing three things that you stand for, what would it say?

2. If you could spend one day with any person who ever lived who would it be and why?

3. Think of an animal that represents your strengths and characteristics and write down why.

4. If you could have one prayer answered, what would it be and why?

5. Describe a time when you felt real strong about a cause or issue. What do you think this says about your values?

6. Your school newspaper is doing a story on you, what would you want the headline of your story to be?

7. If you could solve one problem for the world what would it be and why?

The answers to these questions will provide you with information about yourself that will enable you to get clear about what it is you value. Remember, "Stand for something or you'll fall for anything."

Power Move #18
Take Control of Your Time

How many times have you waited until the last minute to study for a test or work on an important project, only to feel rushed and pressured by having to complete a large amount of work in a short amount of time? If you are like most people who procrastinate you probably even make excuses for your last minute antics by saying things like, "I work better under pressure." But the truth is we do not, because if we are trying to throw things together at the last minute worrying about whether or not we can pull it off, then we are not working at our best potential.

I know what you're thinking. You've got a lot of things on your plate and there is no way that you can manage it all. Believe it or not, managing your time makes life easier. Why? Because managing your time and setting priorities can help you do all the things you need to do and still have time left over for yourself. The better you organize your life, the more you'll be able to do with it. This means more time for friends and family, more time to devote to your schoolwork and more time for you to do the things that you enjoy.

In order to manage your time more effectively, get yourself a planner that organizes your time weekly and daily. Take fifteen minutes on Sunday or Monday morning to plan your week and write down the important things you need to do each day. Once you've planned your schedule for the week, you can adjust it each day as needed.

The great thing about a planner is it will help you remember important things like: appointments, telephone numbers, email addresses and friend's birthdays. The bottom line is successful people take control of their time by planning their schedule. The more effectively you manage your time, the more time you'll have to do the things that you truly enjoy.

Power Move #19
Strive to Make a Difference

Believe it or not, one person can make a difference. I was speaking to a group of teens at a youth leadership conference, when a teenager in the audience shared a story about a program called "Suitcases for Kids." The story goes, that one day a young girl heard that kids in foster care carried their clothes and personal belongings around in garbage bags. The young girl was so disturbed by this, that she started a campaign to get people to donate their suitcases to youth in the foster care system. As a result, "Suitcases for Kids" was created. This example proves that one person can make a difference.

Many people believe that it takes a lot of time and money to make a difference, but that's not true. All it takes is an open mind and a willing heart. You can make a difference every time you walk out your door, by being thoughtful, helpful, kind and compassionate. Giving up your seat on the subway or bus for someone who's older, disabled or pregnant is one way that you can make a difference. Offering to help an elderly person with their groceries or a mother carry her stroller up a flight of stairs are some other ways that you can make a difference. Helping around the house without your parents having to ask you, is another way that you can make a difference. A simple smile can make a big difference to someone who's feeling down.

Every time you help someone in need, stand up for someone who is unable to stand up for themselves, do what is right despite what other people think, or let someone know how much you appreciate them, you are making a difference. Can you imagine how much better off we all would be if each of us made it a point to make a difference? The good news is you can make the world a better place, just by choosing to make a difference.

Power Move #20
Get a Life

How you spend your free time, says a lot about how serious you are about making it. Do you watch television or music videos day in and day out or play video games from the time you get home from school until the time you go to bed? Do you hang on the corner every day without a real sense of purpose? Don't get me wrong, there is nothing wrong with watching television, playing video games, or hanging out with friends, but you should also get involved in structured activities like: sports, martial arts, dance, a teen recreation program or, any other positive activity that helps you to learn and grow. Why is it important to get involved in structured activities? Because as you and I both know, there are a lot of things that can easily knock you off course like: drugs, gangs and negative friends. The more time you spend participating in positive activities that you enjoy, the less time you have to get caught up in negativity.

Here are some questions that will help you find positive outlets for your free time.

1. What do you absolutely love to do? List at least 5 things that you love to do. It could be singing, writing, rapping, drawing, reading, or looking at magazines.

2. What do you need to improve? List at least three things you need to improve. It could be your math grades, English, Science, an attitude.

3. Is there a club or group that you would like to join or start?

4. What programs for teens exist in your neighborhood? In your school?

5. What adults can you talk to, to find out what's going on for teens? A teacher? A counselor? Your parents? Your friend's parents?

By answering these questions, you have empowered yourself with information about your hobbies, clubs for teens and programs for teens. Now find something positive to do and get to it.

Power Move #21
Be Smart About Money

If you are like most people, you want your money to go a long way. You want to be able to buy the things you need and maybe even have a little left over for a rainy day. The key to making your money work for you is to plan wisely. Whatever type of lifestyle you want to live, you can make it happen if you plan for it. The time to plan is now so that you'll be able to live your desired lifestyle when you get older.

No matter how small your income, you can begin managing your money. Whether you have a part-time babysitting job, work at McDonalds or you get an allowance, you can begin developing good money management habits right now. A spending plan will help you make your money go a long way. What is a spending plan? A spending plan is a plan that helps you spend and save wisely. It helps you to become more disciplined about your spending habits so that your money buys all the things you need and some of the things you want. It allows you to see where your money goes and how far your money goes. In essence, a spending plan helps you keep track of your money.

If you are like most people, I'll bet that you've been in situations where you had $5, $10 or even $25 in your pocket but by the end of the day you could not remember what you did with it. Most of us have been in this predicament, but a spending plan would have helped you to figure out exactly where your money went.

Here are five steps that will help you develop better money management habits.

1. *Make a Guesstimate of How Much Money You Take In*
    A good money management plan begins by identifying your income, how much money you take in.

Your income may be a salary from a job, a regular allowance or stipend, money you make from using your talents like cooking, sewing or styling hair. To keep track of how much money you have coming in each month, you'll need to write it down in a book. If you receive your income once a week then multiply that number by four, to get your monthly income.

2. **Make A Guesstimate of How Much You Spend**
In order to get a clearer picture of how much money you spend each month write down all of your expenses. This includes: rent, telephone, groceries, credit card payments, car payments, money that you may have to give your parents towards household expenses and tuition for school. Your expenses also includes things like: clothing, entertainment, CD's, hair and nails, make-up, junk food and other items that you spend your money on.

3. **Subtract Your Total Expenses From Your Total Income**
Once you know what you are taking in (*income*) and what you are spending out (*expenses*) you should subtract the total expenses for the month from the total income for the month. If you are taking in more than you are spending then you are way ahead of the game, because now you can start putting some money away for the future. If you are spending more than you are earning, then you have to figure out a way to increase your income or cut down on your expenses. If this is the case, go back to your list of expenses and see what you can cut back on like: your cell phone, pager, weekly manicures. You should also limit the use of your credit cards.

4. **Set Up A Budget**
If you are spending more than you are earning the solution is not to totally stop doing the things you love, it's making smarter choices concerning how you spend your money.

Look at small ways that you can cut back on your expenses. Do you really need a cell phone? If the answer is yes, get a prepaid one. Can you get your hair and nails done once every three weeks instead of every week? Setting up a budget means determining how much you will spend each month and sticking to it. It will help you live within your means and eventually save up enough to live your desired lifestyle.

5. *Save As Much As You Can*

If you have dreams of buying a nice car, owning a home or starting a business you need to start saving now. I know what you're thinking. "I'm young, I have plenty of time and I barely make enough to buy a happy meal at McDonalds." Believe me; this will pay off for you in the long run. From your first pay check or from your current allowance start saving. Even if you put away $1.00 a week, it will pay off in the long run. By putting aside a little bit of money each time you get paid, you are building a financial nest egg for yourself.

Power Move #22
Increase Your Earning Potential
By Increasing Your Value

What does it mean to increase your value? It means to position yourself in a way where you are viewed as a valuable person who has the ability to make a significant contribution to any job, program, school, club or organization. Three major ways that you can increase your value are: develop your skills, nurture your talents and make learning a lifelong commitment.

Every day, look for ways to expand your skills, knowledge and talents. You will not only prosper financially, but intellectually and emotionally as well. Get as much education as you can from a variety of sources. Don't limit your education to the classroom. Instead become a student of life. Whether it's a college degree, vocational or technical training, an apprenticeship or hands-on learning through an internship or volunteer program, learn as much as you can. Here are 12 ways to increase your value.

1) Watch the Biography or Discovery channel.
2) Listen to the news or read the newspaper.
3) Go to the library and read different kinds of books.
4) Trace your family history and create a family tree.
5) Learn to play chess.
6) Go to the museum or an art gallery.
7) Go to a play or the ballet.
8) Join a debate team.
9) Participate more in class.
10) Give a speech about something that you strongly believe in.
11) Get together with some friends and create a documentary.
12) Talk to people who are doing what you want to do.

Power Move#23
Develop a Prosperity Mindset

As strange as this may sound, the road to prosperity does not begin with creating a spending plan, opening a savings account or even stashing money away in your secret hiding place. It begins in your heart and mind. How you think and feel about money, determines to a large extent how prosperous you become. True prosperity is not about how much money you have, it's about being grateful for the little things, feeling rich on the inside and living a purpose-driven life. This is why prosperity begins in the heart and mind then extends to your pockets. And the quickest way to make your pockets reflect the richness that's inside of you, is to make the most of who you are. Put your talents to good use and give back. Genesis 1:28 speaks to this truth by saying, "be fruitful and multiply." I believe that this passage does not only mean to carry on the human race but also to multiply everything we have including our talents, skills, and resources.

The spiritual law of reaping and sowing teaches that what we put forth is what we get back. It also teaches that in order to receive we must give. Why? Because giving is what keeps the cycle of abundance flowing in our lives. This does not mean that you should give your money away foolishly. It means that you should invest and donate a portion of your income to your place of worship, an organization that helps others or a cause that you believe in so that people who are unable to care for themselves like the sick, homeless and hungry will be able to be cared for. If you do not have any income to donate, you can always donate food, clothes that you no longer wear or your time.

True wealth is not about how much money you have. It's about utilizing all of your potential to create a rich and fruitful life.

Power Move #24
Be Your Neighbor's Keeper

Imagine for a moment that you were beaten and mugged. When it was over you asked two people who happened to be sitting directly across from you if they saw what happened. They said no and continued talking to each other as if nothing happened. But you knew deep in your heart that from where they were sitting they had to have seen something. You then ask if they could spare some change so you can call home. They tell you that they don't have any spare change. They ask you to stop bothering them. Then walk away.

You sit on the bench and begin to cry and no one stops to help you. To make matters worse you can't even call home to ask your parents to come get you, because you don't have any money on you. Then finally, someone stops and asks you, "What's wrong." You tell them what happened. They call the police then your parents and wait with you until your parents arrive. You feel safe and cared for. You are grateful that somebody stopped to help you. And to top it all off, this person didn't even know you. He or she was just being neighborly.

While this is an extreme example and I would never want you to do anything that would jeopardize your own safety, it is important that we as human beings watch out for one another. There comes a time when we have to stop thinking only of ourselves and start thinking about other people. While you should never get directly involved in an incident that could put you in immediate danger, there is no reason why you can't go to a pay phone, place an anonymous call to the police, describe what you saw and hang up.

If you have an elderly neighbor you can volunteer to do her grocery shopping or run errands. You can visit the sick or volunteer at your local community center.

There are a number of ways that you can be your neighbor's keeper. You can:

- Start a neighborhood youth watch.
- Stand up for the underdog.
- Give a homeless person some spare change.
- Read a book to a child who's in the hospital.
- Donate some of your old clothes to someone less fortunate than you.

It is our spiritual and social responsibility to look out for one another. Every time you help someone else, it's like making a deposit in the universal bank of blessings. And when you are in need of a blessing, you can rest assured that someone will come your way to help you.

Power Move#25
Be a Positive Role Model

Has it ever occurred to you that you may be the only positive influence on someone else's life? Have you ever stopped to think that you may be the only example of excellence and integrity to a classmate, neighbor or friend? As strange as it may seem, people are always watching you, even if you are not aware of it. And the more you do what's right, the more your peers will look to you as a positive role model. They may never tell you. They may never admit it to themselves. They may even make fun of you for being the type of person who tries to do what is right, but that does not mean that they do not respect you or look up to you.

When you have a vision of something greater for your life and work towards that vision you will become a positive role model for others whether you want to or not. When you value, believe in and respect yourself, people will notice that there's something different about you. And chances are you will not fit in with everyone else. That's a good thing, because it means that you are unique and you were given the special task of being a beacon of light for others.

Being a role model isn't always easy. There will be times when you will find yourself at odds with your friends. You'll even worry about fitting in. Don't worry. You're not supposed to fit in. Being a role model means that you stand out for others to see. There is something special about knowing that you are trying to set a good example and that you care enough to be the very best. Whether or not you are popular has nothing to do with being a role model. A role model is someone who chooses to put forth their best effort everyday and when they make a mistake they pick themselves up and try again. If this sounds like you, then I say that you are a positive role model. Keep up the good work.

Power Move#26
Don't Be Wrong and Strong

In other words, admit when you are wrong. No one is right 100% of the time, not even you. It never ceases to amaze me when I see someone bump into someone else on the subway or in a crowded elevator, then look at the person who they bumped into with an attitude as if the person they bumped should apologize. How dare any of us wrong someone else and not take responsibility for our behavior, whether it was intentional or not.

When we fail to acknowledge our wrong behavior what we are really saying is, "I am too immature and small-minded to admit when I'm wrong." Think about all the energy that it takes to defend yourself and try to prove how right you are when you are the one at fault. Think about all the arguing and stress that goes along with defending your position even when you know you are dead wrong. Not only is this a waste of time, it's completely nuts.

Imagine how much easier life would be if you could admit when you are wrong and move forward. Admitting that you are wrong when you are at fault is not a sign of weakness, it is an indication of courage and maturity. Any fool can be wrong and strong, but it takes a person of integrity and high moral character to admit when they are wrong. What type of person will you choose to be?

Power Move #27
Learn to Forgive

When someone does something to upset you, ask yourself, "Why am I really upset?" Is it because I trusted someone, who I should not have trusted in the first place? Did I expect something of someone that they were not ready or able to give? Did I make more out of a situation than what actually happened? Am I blowing things out of proportion? If you answered yes to any of these questions, then the person you need to forgive is you. Forgive yourself for being human and move on. If the answer is no, then forgive the person who wronged you so that you can move forward.

Forgiveness is not something you do for someone else; it is something that you do for yourself so that you don't become bitter and resentful. See, the longer you hold on to negative feelings the more you become consumed by them. This prevents you from being happy and whole. While the person who wronged you has moved on and is not even thinking about what he/she did, you are still tied to the pain of that experience and believe it or not you're still tied to that person. This is why it is so important to forgive. The power of forgiveness allows us to let go of negative feelings and free ourselves from anger and resentment. Holding on to negative feelings towards someone else robs us of our peace of mind and happiness. By forgiving someone who has wronged you, you give yourself the chance to heal and grow.

Some people confuse forgiveness with being a doormat or allowing people to get away with mistreating you. This is not forgiveness. You can forgive someone and still want to see justice (not revenge). You can forgive someone and still choose not to have a relationship with him/her, especially if the relationship causes you more harm than good. Forgiveness does not necessarily mean reconciliation. You may never see the person again but you can still choose to forgive them in your heart. Forgiveness simply means, making the choice not to allow someone else's mistreatment of you to fill your heart with bitterness or prevent you from living a happy, successful life.

Believe it or not, one of the keys to a long and healthy life is being able to forgive, Start with a clean slate. Choose to forgive.

Power Move #28
Treat Your Mind Like an Apartment

The single most important thing that you can do to keep a positive attitude is, take control of your thoughts. While you cannot control every thought that comes into your mind, you can certainly choose not to dwell on the negative ones. This is what I call, treating your mind like an apartment.

When you treat your mind like an apartment you become the landlord and your thoughts become the tenants. As the landlord of your mind, whenever you have a tenant who is not paying rent (a negative thought) it is up to you to evict that tenant. Whatever you believe with certainty eventually becomes your reality, because we always act in ways that support our truest beliefs. The more attention that you give to a belief, the more likely that belief will shape the choices you make. This is why it is so important that you eliminate negative thinking.

Try to identify the negative thoughts that are preventing you from reaching your goals and that are holding you back in any way. Once you have identified those thoughts, replace them with more positive realistic ones. Here are some examples of how you can change a negative thought into a more positive, realistic one.

Negative Thought
I have no friends. Nobody likes me.

Positive Thought
There are a lot of great people who would like to be friends with me. If I get involved in activities that I enjoy, I will meet new people who I can build friendships with.

Negative Thought
I'm not good at anything. I have no talent.

Positive Thought
Everyone has a talent. If I try different things that I find interesting I will discover what I'm good at.

These are just two examples of how you can change a negative thought into a more positive, realistic one.

The truth is you can turn any negative thought into a positive one, by choosing to focus on the positive. And over time your actions will become consistent with the new beliefs that you've chosen to adopt. The messages we carry around in our heads are powerful. You can choose to use this power for your betterment just by adopting a positive mindset. It's your mind. Take charge of it!

Power Move #29
Don't Believe the Hype

There are some people who believe all of the negativity that they see and hear about teenagers. They hear stories about school shootings, gang violence and teenage drug use and put all teenagers in the same category. While there is a segment of the teen population who engage in negative activities, the large majority of teens do not. Each year thousands of teenagers complete high school, go on to college, hold down jobs and live successful lives. There are lots of teenagers just like you, who are taking positive steps in the right direction.

So the question is, whose report are you going to believe? Does it matter to you that you have the God-given right, to glorify and magnify all that you were born with and capable of achieving? Does it matter to you that the fact that you are still here means that you are a survivor? Does it matter to you that you were genetically coded for greatness? Does it matter to you that just by nature of reading this book you are on the right track? Or does it only matter to you what other people? Don't believe the hype. You can do anything you set your mind to.

Fear, lack of confidence and media brainwashing can make you believe that things are hopeless for you. But they are not. There is a great big world waiting for you to leave your mark in a positive way. What you have to do is tune out the negative messages and tune into the positive ones. Don't doubt yourself. Don't let other people's negative opinions become your own. Do not look for the worst in yourself or others. And whatever you do, don't believe the hype.

Power Move #30
Don't Sweat the Small Stuff, Especially Small People

Why is it that so many people focus their time and energy on people and things that really don't matter? We live in a fast-paced and stressful society. We compound that level of stress when we sweat trivial things and trivial people. It takes strength of character and emotional maturity to let things go. What you need to realize is, when you get bent out of shape over little things, when you become easily irritated and when you overreact over the tiniest little, annoyances, you're the one who becomes stressed out and upset. When you lose control and get puffed up over things that don't really matter, you waste precious energy that could be better used working towards your goals and living a happy life.

In short, sweating the small stuff while trying to succeed in life is a big waste of time. Why? Because your own frustrations and reactions will get in the way of your success. You'll become your own worst enemy because you will live your life reacting and responding to small situations and small people instead of taking control of what gets your time and attention. When you learn how to stop sweating the small stuff, you will become happier and more at peace with yourself. Life's small annoyances won't go away, but you'll respond to them with more confidence and control.

It is not hard to understand why most people sweat the small stuff; people can really work your nerves and inconvenient occurrences can sometimes get the best of you. For example, you're on line at the supermarket and the cashier is really slow, or you just got a new haircut and one of your classmates has something smart to say about it. These things can be annoying, but they shouldn't make you lose your cool.

Can you imagine how happier your life would be if you learned to sweat the small stuff a little less often? Your life would not be perfect, but you wouldn't get upset as often. You would get along with your friends better than you already do and annoying situations wouldn't bother you as much. That sounds like a happier life to me. Doesn't it?

There's no question that people will do things to upset you and uncontrollable events will come you way, but if you could learn not to make a big deal out of the little things and sometimes even the big things, your life will become easier to manage.

Power Move #31
Don't Let Fear Hold You Back

Some people say that *FEAR* stands for *False Evidence Appearing Real.* Others say it's *False Education Accepted As Reality.* One thing I know for certain is fear can hold you back from living up to your full potential and becoming all that you were meant to be. Far too often, fear is the only thing that stands in the way of your ability to achieve your goals. We come into this world with only two fears: the fear of falling and the fear of loud noises. All other fears are learned responses.

Fear can help us become more alert when we sense danger, this is called the fight or flight response. It is a natural survival instinct that kicks in when we believe that we are in danger. The problem comes in when our fear response is not related to any real danger; such as fear of failure or fear of looking stupid. These types of fears can cause you to unintentionally sabotage your success. For example, let's say that you have a natural talent for singing and you want to be a singer, but you are afraid to perform in front of other people. So instead of going out and performing for the public you only sing in the shower, thus decreasing your chances of being discovered. Or suppose you want to try out for the school play, but you are afraid that your friends will think that you're corny. So you never audition. By not auditioning you are holding yourself back from exploring your artistic side. As you can see, fear can cause you to go through life sabotaging your chances of success.

Fear discourages us from living our dreams and it makes us give up on going after what we really want in life. Whenever you feel fearful of trying something new or difficult, remind yourself that you have nothing to be afraid of. When that doesn't work feel the fear and do it anyway. Put fear in its proper perspective. You cannot fail in life if you follow your dreams, go after your goals and try something new.

Power Move #32
Listen Up

It's been said that we have two ears and one mouth so that we can listen twice as much as we speak. Listening is a skill that is developed with practice and patience. To truly understand someone you must listen to them. The problem is that most people don't know how to listen. Often when we should be listening we give unsolicited advice, tell the other person why they shouldn't feel the way they feel or we completely zone out.

Have you ever tried to tell someone something really important that was going on in your life and they either cut you off in mid sentence or were too distracted to give you their full attention? How did that make you feel? My guess is you felt disrespected. Well, that's what happens when you do not practice full listening. The person who is doing the talking feels disrespected. They feel like you don't care.

When you automatically give unsolicited advice, constantly interrupt the other person, or completely tune them out, what you are really saying is, "I'm not paying attention to you." And when people feel like you are not interested in hearing what they have to say or you're simply not willing to take the time to listen, they will eventually stop talking to you. And you may end up missing out on important information or losing a friend.

To hear what another person is truly saying, you need to listen with your eyes, ears and heart. Pay attention to the words they use, their facial expressions, tone of voice and body language. Don't make assumptions based on how you see things. And don't behave like a know-it-all. Just pay attention and really try to understand where the other person is coming from. Try to stand in their shoes. To become a good listener, you need to imagine what it would be like to be in the other person's situation. And you must try to see the world as they see it.

To make sure that you understand the other person, it's a good idea to summarize their words. This means you should repeat what the other person has said to you. This allows the other person to know that you heard what they said and it gives them an opportunity to clear up any misunderstandings.

Listening is difficult in itself, because as humans we become easily distracted. Throw your parents in the mix and it's virtually impossible. Why? Because you are used to tuning them out.

If you want to improve your relationship with your parents and shock them at the same time, try listening to them with full attention. It may seem strange at first, but the next time your mom or dad talks to you about your grades, choice of friends, household chores or anything else you wish they would leave you alone about, stop for a minute and really try to understand where they are coming from. If they feel like you listen to them, then they will be more likely to listen to you. Seems like a win/win situation. Right?

One more thing: once you get really good at listening with full attention, share the benefits of this power move with everyone you know.

Power Move #33
Give Yourself What You Give to Others

Are you the type of person who is always there when someone needs you? You know just what to say to lift someone up when they are feeling down. You know just what to do to help a friend through a difficult situation. With a kind word, a smile, some well thought-out advice, or an action plan you're able to help someone in need get on the right track. You're known as the guy or girl who others can depend on when they need a helping hand. You're always there to give, sometimes to your own detriment.

Giving is a noble thing. It's good for the soul, especially in today's times when most people are consumed with trying to see what they can get. But while you are giving to others make sure you stop along the way to give yourself. Give yourself love, encouragement and support. And when you can't give these things to yourself seek out people who can give these things to you. Everyone, even you, needs a little tender love and care every now and then. It's important to take time for yourself, to relax and recharge. If you don't, you will burn yourself out. There are many ways that you can relax and recharge. You can:

- Go for a long walk and clear your thoughts
- Visit a garden and escape from the stress of everyday life.
- Have a good cry and release overwhelming emotions.
- Read a good book.
- Watch a funny movie.
- Take a long, relaxing bath.
- Join a youth group.
- Pray or meditate.
- Write a poem or read one.
- Go to the beach.
- Write your thoughts in a journal.

In the space below write down some other things that you can do to give yourself what you give to others.

_____
_____
_____
_____
_____
_____
_____
_____
_____
_____
_____
_____
_____
_____
_____
_____
_____
_____
_____
_____
_____
_____
_____
_____
_____
_____

Power Move #34
Keep It Real

Since so many of you are quick to say that you "keep it real," I'd like to clarify what keeping it real really means. Keeping it real does not mean spitting in the street or grabbing your crotch in public; that's keeping it obscene. Keeping it real does not mean yelling at your parents, cursing out your teachers or talking to adults as if they were your peers; that's keeping it disrespectful. Keeping it real does not mean smoking blunts and drinking 40's; that's keeping it addicted. Keeping it real does not mean being promiscuous and practicing unsafe sex, that's keeping it lethal. Keeping it real does not mean performing below your academic potential or cutting class; that's keeping it stupid. And finally keeping it real does not mean robbing, selling drugs or assaulting people; that's keeping it criminal.

So the question remains "what does keeping it real really mean?" Rejecting the wildly popular notion that keeping it real means saying and doing whatever you feel, whenever you feel, however you feel; I believe that keeping it real means being genuine, honest, trustworthy and treating others with tact and sincerity. For me, keeping it real is doing what you know is right despite what other people are doing.

Keeping it real means doing your best to live righteously. In the African-American culture there is a code of conduct based on the Egyptian code of MAAT that promotes genuineness and harmony. In essence, it helps those who follow it to keep things real. I'd like to share these principles with you. I believe the code of MAAT will help you to always, keep it real. Here is the code of MAAT.

1) *Truth*- to seek truth, speak truth and accept truth.

2) **Righteousness**-to do what is right in order to create balance and harmony.

3) **Justice**-to treat others as you would have them treat you.

4) **Harmony**-to think and act in ways that manifest peace, cooperation and accord.

5) **Balance**-to strive for stability and a state of equilibrium.

6) **Propriety**-to be humble and speak with a conscious tongue.

7) **Order**-to be organized and clear. To be consciously aware that there is a divine system at work.

When you adopt these principles and practice them consistently, you will be able to keep it real. Please take a few moments to write down some other ways that you can keep it real.

_____

_____

_____

_____

_____

_____

_____

_____

_____

_____

_____

_____

Power Move #35
Keep Your Parents In The Mix

I know. You're probably thinking: *"keep my parents in the mix, I'd like to keep them as far away from my private life as possible."* As a teenager, you may find that your relationship with your parents is more intense than ever before. Perhaps you argue about things that you never fought over before. Or maybe, your parents ask more questions about who you're hanging out with, where you're going and what your interests are. Your parents may be surprised by your new views and choices and how fast you're growing and changing. But don't let your quest to exert your independence make you shut your parents out. Keep the lines of communication open and let them know by your actions that they can trust you and count on you to do what's right.

Believe it or not, your parents want the best for you; even if they never say or show it. The reason they ask so many questions and seem like they're always trying to get in your business is not because they are nosey (well, maybe just a little) it's because they love you and want to keep you out of harms way. They know what it's like to be a teenager and they know the challenges that lie ahead of you. They want to protect you and prevent you from making some of the mistakes that they made when they were your age.

As strange as it may seem, your parents have pressures too. While you are worrying about fitting in with your friends, whether or not that cute guy or girl at school likes you, they are worrying about keeping a roof over your head and keeping you safe in a fast-paced world. Just like you, they have days where they feel overwhelmed, unappreciated and defeated. They may have had to sacrifice some of their dreams in order to create a better life for you.

As a teenager, I spent so much time being angry with my mom that I never took the time to recognize how much she had to sacrifice to create a better life for me. There were days when she wanted to buy something nice for herself, but she could not because she had to feed and clothe me. There were days when she wanted to go out by herself but she could not because she had to take care of me. Your parents are people too. They won't always get things right. Sometimes they will completely screw up, just like you and me. But if you keep the lines of communication open, you will develop a better relationship with your parents.

And truthfully speaking, if you get caught up in a difficult situation, it will be your parents who will more often than not have to bail you out. And in order for them to help you, they need to know what they are dealing with. Keeping your parents in the mix ensures that they will be able to help you out if you get into trouble. Let's say you're at a friend's house but you lied and told your parents that you were going to the library. Your friend has a few drinks and the two of you decide to drive over to another friend's house. You get into an accident and are taken to the nearest hospital. Your identification gets lost in the process. The doctor has no way to contact your parents and your parents have no reason to contact the hospital because they believe that you're at the library. What do you do? This whole scenario may have been avoided if you told your parents where you were really going in the first place.

Keeping your parents in the mix makes good sense. If they feel that you are attempting to build a close relationship with them, then they'll be much more willing to listen to you, they'll trust you more and they'll be more willing to compromise.

Power Move #36
Accentuate the Positive

Accentuating the positive means displaying your natural talents and letting others see the best you have to offer. An important part of accentuating the positive is discovering what you are good at. One thing I've learned is that everyone has a talent. Everyone has something that they do well. Identify your gifts and talents and allow them to shine.

When you accentuate the positive you are letting it be known that you care enough about yourself to put your best effort forward. So pick up those books and show your teachers how smart you are. Pick up the iron and iron those clothes. Walk upright and strut your stuff with poise and confidence. Dress neatly, develop good hygiene habits and let the real you shine through.

Get to know yourself; your likes, dislikes, strengths, and weaknesses, then put your best foot forward. I'm not saying to be conceited or to turn yourself into an overblown egomaniac, just step it up a notch so that others can see how truly special and gifted you are.

What separates ordinary people from extraordinary ones? Extraordinary people accentuate the positive. So go out and work it, then sit back and watch how much your life changes for the better.

Write down five ways that you can accentuate the positive.

1. _____
2. _____
3. _____
4. _____
5. _____

Power Move #37
Develop An Attitude of Gratitude

Developing an attitude of gratitude means learning to be thankful for what you have, even if you don't have everything that you want. It means appreciating the simple things and being grateful for the good in your life. If you learn to be thankful for the little things, you will soon come to realize how blessed you truly are no matter what your situation.

The conscious acknowledgment of what's good in your life will help you to persevere when life's storms come your way. Instead of being defeated by life's challenges, you'll be able to keep moving forward because you'll know that no matter how bad things seem as long as you are alive, there's hope for a better tomorrow. When you give thanks each day for what you have, you make room for more blessings to come into your life.

Begin your attitude of gratitude today. Find a notebook and write down three things that you are grateful for. You can write down anything that you feel grateful for. For example, if a friend treats you to a slice of pizza, if you pass a difficult exam, if you find $1 in your jacket pocket, these are all things that you can write down in your book. Everyday write down at least three things that you are grateful for. Start a gratitude contest with a group of friends and come up with a prize at the end of each month for the person who writes down the most things that he/she is grateful for.

As time passes and you fill your notebook with things that you are grateful for, you will see how rich your life really is. Think of your gratitude entries as a daily thank you note to life.

Today I am grateful for...

_____

_____

Power Move #38
Don't Let Adversity Defeat You

Life is full of challenges and struggles. But without challenges, you really can't tell what you're made of. And without struggle you cannot develop the strength of character to persevere in life. No one likes adversity, but adversity does not have to defeat you if you stand firm in the face of it. Adversity happens to all of us. Everyone experiences difficult situations and setbacks. It is during these times that you have to dig deep within yourself and pull out your inner courage. You can come through adversity stronger and wiser if you do not allow yourself to be defeated by it.

During the most challenging times you must know that if others have risen above adversity you can too. Don't let yourself become defeated, just keep moving forward. And if you keep on keeping on, you will survive. One thing I know for certain is that storms don't last forever. Eventually the sun will come out. When I was growing up, the old folks used to say, "This too shall pass." What this saying means is, no matter how bad the situation, it won't last forever. You can take great comfort in knowing that all of life's storms eventually pass. But what determines how you come through your challenge is what you do while you are going through.

Some of our greatest lessons in life come from adversity. If you develop the attitude that every problem or challenge is an opportunity to grow, then setbacks will only prepare you for greater comebacks. *What important life lessons have you learned from adversity?*

_____

_____

Power Move #39
Get Connected

Supportive relationships with caring adults are key to your success. Having adults in your life to motivate you to keep moving forward, encourage you to go for your dreams, push you beyond your comfort zone, and get on your case when you need it, can make a big difference in how far you go in life. Every teen needs a supportive and caring adult who they can talk to from time to time. The more adults you have in your life to encourage and support you, the greater your chances of reaching your goals.

Having a network of positive adults provides you with the additional support, and resources that are necessary for going far in life. This is why you need to connect with supportive and caring adults. There are many ways to connect with positive adults. Here are some suggestions.

- Talk to your favorite teacher after class and let him/her know what your goals are. Ask him/her if you can meet or speak by telephone on a regular basis to map out your goals.

- Ask one of your parent's friends to teach you something that you've always wanted to learn.

- Start a club for youth who would like to adopt a mentor. Tell every adult you know about your club until you find yourself a mentor. Consider talking to an adult from your church, a teacher or an adult who works in your community.

- Start a youth council in your school, community center or in your neighborhood. Meet with the adults in these institutions on a regular basis. Let them know what your needs are and how they can support you.

By connecting with positive adults you give yourself a head start on success. There are many adults who are sincere about investing in youth. If you let them know that you are serious, then they will go out of their way to help you.

In the space below write down the names of five adults who you can connect with.

1. _____

2. _____

3. _____

4. _____

5. _____

Power Move #40
Take Care of Your Body

Taking care of your body means doing all that you can to stay in good physical health. This includes regular exercise, good eating habits, adequate rest and developing a positive body image. The time to care for your body is now while you are young and healthy, so that you will remain in good health as you grow older. In short, your body is your temple and if you want it to serve you well you have to take good care of it.

We've all heard the expression "you are what you eat." And for the most part this is true. Some of you may already have healthy eating habits, while others are literally killing themselves with junk food or by not eating regularly. You can improve your diet immediately just by eating less fast food, chips and sweets and eating more wholesome foods like: fruits and vegetables, poultry, fish, whole-grain breads, cereal and dairy. Also, be sure to drink plenty of water, 6 to 8 glasses per day. By improving your diet just a little you improve your health a whole lot.

Another important element of good health is regular physical activity. Exercise and sports not only enhances one's physical stamina, they help to reduce stress. Choose an activity you like and incorporate it into your weekly regimen. Make time for exercise, at least three days per week. There's no single best way to exercise, just do something that you like. The payoff is you will look and feel better.

Getting adequate rest is another key ingredient to good physical health. You need seven to ten hours of rest per day, yet most teens get half of that amount. Remember your body is like a machine. It needs tune-ups, fuel and rest. Make a commitment to good health by taking care of your body and you'll reap the benefits of a long and healthy life.

Power Move #41
Care for Your Soul

Just as you care for your mind and body you need to care for your soul. I call this being spiritually fit. Your soul is a very private and personal area of your life and there are many ways to care for it. Taking good care of your soul is about nurturing your inner self, reflecting on your life and most importantly, developing a personal relationship with the Creator. Here are some things you can do to care for your soul:

1) *Talk to God*- ask for strength, courage, guidance or share whatever is on your mind.
2) *Meditate*- Clear your mind and listen to what that still, small voice is saying to you.
3) *Serve others*- do something nice for someone who is less fortunate than you.
4) *Write in a Journal*- Write down your deepest thoughts and inner most feelings.
5) *Go for A Nature Walk*- Take a stroll down a garden, the beach, a nearby park, a river and take in the glory of nature.

There is no right or wrong way to care for your soul. What is most important is that you feel more spiritually fulfilled and uplifted as a result of caring for your soul. Please take a few moments and write down some other ways that you can care for your soul. I can care for my soul by:

_____
_____
_____

Power Move #42
Speak Up

Every person has basic human rights and as a teenager you have basic rights too. They key is, knowing what your rights are so that you can advocate for yourself. Knowing your rights will not only help you to stand up for yourself, it will enable you to get more involved in the betterment of your community so that you can stand up for issues that you strongly believe in.

Below are some of your rights and responsibilities. Review them, learn them and protect them. You have the right to:

- Be protected from physical, emotional and sexual abuse and neglect.
- Voice your feelings and be heard.
- Be respected by others.
- Talk with an adult you trust if someone is abusing or mistreating you.
- Have privacy.
- Take charge of your life.
- Say no to unreasonable requests and things that make you feel uncomfortable.
- To love, be happy and pursue your dreams.
- Food, shelter, clothing, medical care and an education.

The Do's and Don't of Advocacy

Do know that you have the right to stand up for yourself.
Don't let fear prevent you from speaking up.
Do ask an adult you trust to help you.
Don't feel like you're being a pest when you ask for help.
Do be honest about what you're advocating for.
Don't think that you do not have power. You do.

Power Move #43
Be Job Ready

How do you become job ready? You become job ready by making the conscious effort to develop the skills, habits, and attitude that will enable you to get and keep a job. Often when teens think of getting a job, they don't think about the skills and attitudes that are necessary to not only get the job but to keep it. Whether you want a part time job, a summer job or you need to work full time while attending college, there is intense competition for good paying jobs. The more you bring to the table in terms of your attitude, habits, and skills, the greater your chances of getting the job you want.

One of the very first questions that potential employers will ask is, "why should we hire you?" You have to be able to answer that question by demonstrating that you are the best candidate for the job. You need to convince your potential employer that what you lack in training and experience, you make up for with your enthusiasm, work ethic and willingness to learn.

More often than not a non-paid internship or a volunteer position can be just as beneficial as a paid position. Why? Because it provides you with an opportunity to gain work experience, develop specific skills, make valuable contacts, and learn how things work in the real world. Once you develop these skills and resources, you can later use them to obtain a paying job. Keep in mind that payment is not limited to money. Valuable contacts that you can later use as references are also a form of payment.

In order to think about ways to gain work experience please answer the following questions.

- What type of internships or volunteer positions are
  available in your school, church or youth based agency?

  _____

  _____

- Which of these internships or volunteer opportunities would you like to try out and why?

  _____

  _____

  _____

  _____

  _____

- What steps do you need to take in order to participate in the internship or volunteer opportunity?

  _____

  _____

  _____

  _____

- Do you have a mentor who is working in an industry that you would like to learn more about? Can you help him/her out one afternoon per week?

  _____

  _____

  _____

  _____

Now that you have had an opportunity to think about ways to gain work experience, let's look at the basics of employment readiness. You need to know how to:

1) **Develop A Resume.** A resume is a one to two page description of your work and, or volunteer experience, education, and employment goals. It can include your hobbies, special awards that you've received and any special skills that you have. Talk to you teachers or visit your local library for sample resumes.

2) **Fill out an Application.** Whenever you go on an interview one of the first things you will be asked to do is fill out an employment application. An employment application is used to find out about an applicant's background, work experience, education and references. You can go to your guidance counselor to get a sample employment application or you can get a real application from any fast-food restaurant or retail outlet.

3) **Ace the Interview.** The job interview is an opportunity for the potential employer to find out whether or not you're the right person for the job. It's also your time to find out if the job is right for you. The best way to prepare for an interview is to practice with a caring adult. Let the adult pretend to be the employer and have him/her ask you questions that a potential employer might ask. Take the mock interview seriously and ask for honest feedback. Use the mock interview to prepare for the real thing.

Once you get the job, you have to do your best to keep it. This is the hardest part. Here are some tips that will help you to keep your job.

Tips for Keeping Your Job

- *Be on time* Get to work ten minutes before your work schedule begins. If you are going to be late or absent call ahead of time.

- *Come to work ready to work* You are not being paid to gossip with your friends, daydream about what you're going to do when you leave work or goof off. You are being paid to work.

- *Come to work with a positive attitude* Do not walk around your place of business with a chip on your shoulder. Smile and say hello. Make an effort to get along with the people you work with.

- *Don't get caught up in office drama* Mind your business. Don't bad mouth the people you work with.

- *Don't lose your cool on the job* It's not worth it.

- *Go the extra mile* Do what you can to be a model employee.

- *Put school first* No matter how good the pay is, education should be your #1 priority.

- *If you need to leave a job, do it with tact-* Try to give at least two weeks advance notice. You may have to use this job as a reference one day to get another job. So don't burn bridges with your former employer.

Power Move #44
Learn Something New Each Day

Keep an open mind and learn something new each day. During the teen years you get bombarded with schoolwork, homework, chores and all the other items on your to-do-list, but it is still important to try to learn something new each day. As we discussed earlier, the more information you acquire, the more you increase your value. The more you increase your value, the more you increase your earning potential now and in the future.

Learn one new word each day, read five pages above and beyond your required reading. Watch the history or discovery channel and learn something new. Once you get into the habit of learning one new thing per day, you may be pleasantly surprised to find that you actually enjoy learning just for the sake of expanding your mind.

I used to hate it when adults said to me, "learn something new each day." And you may hate that I am saying this to you. But I can honestly assure you that if you learn as much as you can, you will stand out from the rest and achieve your goals much faster.

Power Move #45
Create Your Own Private Space

Every now and then we all need the comfort of our own private space. It is important to have your own private space, either mentally or physically, where you can go when you need to tune out from the world so that you can tune into yourself. As a writer and motivational speaker, creating my own private space has become a tremendous outlet for me. Going to my own private space, whether I go there in my mind through daydreaming and visualization or whether I go there physically, by taking a nature walk or sifting through an old bookstore, allows me to unwind and do some self-reflection.

Creating your own private space where no one else can get to you spiritually and emotionally is very important. It allows you to be alone and get quiet, think and reflect, meditate and pray, draw and write, sing or be soothed by music. It's a place where you can find peace and comfort and temporarily escape life's problems. It can be your room, the corner of a room, the library, a bookstore, a park, a garden or a place in your mind.

If you do not have a private space where you can relax and be alone with yourself, I strongly encourage you to find one. The best way to find your space is to look around and see what works for you. Take a walk to a nearby beach, lake, river, library, bookstore, garden, museum or park and pay attention to how you feel. If it feels right, then you have probably found the private space that is right for you.

Here are some ways that I can create my own private space. I can...

_____
_____
_____
_____

Power Move #46
Pay Attention to Warning Signs and Wake-up Calls

Suppose that you were presented with a line-up of your friends and were told that one of them has a tendency to get caught up in negative activities. Let's say that you are asked to pick out this person from a line-up. What signs would you look for to indicate whether or not he/she had a tendency to get caught up in negativity? Would you look to see if this person gets high? Would you look to see if this person starts trouble or constantly gets into trouble? Would you look to see if this person is engaged in any activities that you consider harmful and destructive? Well if you look for any of these things what you are really looking for are warning signs.

There are some people who come into your life with warning signs stamped right across their foreheads, but it's up to you to pay attention. Sometimes the warning signs are subtle; like a tiny voice inside of your head telling you that something is not quite right about that person. Sometimes the warning signs are not so subtle; like a nagging voice that won't go away or a trusted adult telling you that there's something about one of your friends that he/she just doesn't like.

Warning signs are present for a very good reason. They are there to protect you from danger. And when you ignore them you usually get yourself into trouble. That little voice inside your head acts like an inner guide prompting you toward your highest good. I believe it's God's voice guiding and protecting you. What I've learned from my inner voice is it's not others who deceive you; it's you who deceives yourself, by not paying attention to the warning signs.

Here are some questions designed to help you get more in tune with your inner voice.

- Name a time that you listened to your intuition and you were glad that you did. What did you learn from the experience?

  _____

  _____

  _____

  _____

- Name a time when you did not listen to your intuition and you regretted it. What did you learn from the experience?

  _____

  _____

  _____

  _____

- Is there a friend or boyfriend/girlfriend that your intuition or a caring adult has been warning you about, but you've dismissed the warnings? What are you going to do?

  _____

  _____

  _____

  _____

- Is there a situation that your intuition or other people are warning you about? What are you going to do?

  _____

  _____

  _____

  _____

  _____

Besides warning signs that protect us from danger there are situations that I refer to as "wake-up calls." Wake-up calls are life-changing situations that affect you so adversely that they force you to wake up and look at the choices you're making so that you can make a change for the better. While most people don't enjoy wake-up calls, sometimes they are necessary to get us back on the right track. Take wake-up calls seriously, because you may not get a second chance.

Wake-up calls can be anything from getting caught stealing, to an argument or fight that gets out of hand, to being suspended from school, to having to go to summer school so that you don't get left back, to finding yourself in any situation that affects you so strongly that it forces you to pay attention to the direction your life is headed in. And two things can happen after a wake-up call. You can learn from the experience and make better decisions or you can keep doing what you're doing until you get yourself in a situation that you cannot get out of. It's your life and it's up to you to decide what you will do when faced with a wake-up call. I hope that you will do the smart thing.

Recall a recent wake-up call that you or someone you know has had. Write down what you learned from the experience.

Power Move #47
Don't Be Ruled By Your Moods

Moody and impulsive are words that many adults use to describe teenagers. I like to say that you are at a stage in your life where you are capable of experiencing and expressing a variety of moods and emotions in a short period of time. Although you have the ability to experience many different moods, be careful not to let your moods rule you. Why? Because no one likes to deal with a moody person. More importantly, if you always give into your moods, then you will lack the focus that you need to be successful.

Think about how deceptive your moods can be. Let's say you are having a bad day and you're really feeling down, your mood can trick you into believing that the situation is much worse than it really is. As a result, you focus your attention on how bad things are rather than seeing the situation for what it really is: a setback, a challenge, or a stressful day.

When you are feeling low, rather than giving into a depressed mood and focusing on everything that's wrong with your life, count your blessings. For each negative thing that you think of, write down two things that you are grateful for. This will allow you to focus on how blessed you are rather than how stressed you are. Also, don't make important decisions while your mood is low, because chances are you won't be able to think clearly. And if the low mood doesn't pass, talk to your parents, a teacher, or counselor.

Not allowing your moods to rule you, is one of the keys to a happy and successful life. If you understand your moods and see them for what they are, you'll save yourself a lot grief and disappointment.

Power Move #48
Respect Yourself and Others

How can you tell if someone really respect themselves? For starters, their day-to-day choices and actions indicate that they value and appreciate themselves as well as have high morals and standards. Further, they conduct themselves with dignity and tact.

Did you know that when you respect yourself, other people respect you too? Why? Because you set the standard. Believe it or not, the way in which you carry yourself has a lot to do with the way other people see and treat you.

A person who has respect for himself/herself: takes pride in his or her appearance by being neat and clean, does not abuse their body by drinking alcohol or using drugs, does not engage in sexual activity until he or she is mature enough to understand the sacredness and responsibility of this act, does not use profanity to express themselves and does not engage in any activity that places them or others in harm's way. How can you build up your self-respect? There are a number of ways that you can build up your self-respect. You can:

- Build a healthy relationship with yourself. Spend time getting to know you and learn to love yourself just as you are.

- Be clear about your values and stand by them.

- Participate in positive activities that nurture your talents.

- Hang out with positive people who reinforce your good feelings about yourself.

In the space below list some other things that you can do to show yourself that you respect yourself.

_____
_____
_____
_____
_____
_____
_____
_____

While it's important to respect yourself, it is also important to respect other people. Everyone has the right to be treated with dignity and respect even if you do not like them. It's really about being big enough to treat other people as you would want them to treat you. And the truth is the more you respect yourself, the more you are able to respect others.

You can demonstrate respect for others by:

- Not cursing at or talking down to other people.

- Not making fun of, spreading rumors about or telling lies on other people.

- Hearing out someone else's opinion even if you disagree.

- Demonstrating good manners by being courteous.

- Listening to your parents, teachers, counselors and other concerned adults without giving them a whole lot of attitude and drama.

Power Move #49
Enjoy Being a Teen

You have your whole life to be an adult. Enjoy being a teen. You've seen the billboards, magazine ads, and commercials promoting everything from casual sex, to smoking and drinking, credit card spending, violent video games and just about everything else under the sun. You've also seen friends and classmates smoking at the mall, wearing highly provocative outfits and doing everything in their power to grow up before their time. You may even feel like tuning out when adults tell you to slow down. Maybe you think that being fast will make you more popular. But in the long run it does not. All it makes you is old before your time.

We live in a world filled with mixed messages. When you are young you're pressured to grow up quickly. When you grow older, you feel pressured to try to stay young. Being a teen is great. It's a time of exploration. You are just where you need to be. This is your time to figure out who you are, where you fit and what you like and dislike. This is your time to begin to set goals and make decisions about your future like: what college you want to go to, what career you want to have and what kind of lifestyle you want to live. This is also the time to make your mistakes, so don't take yourself too seriously.

Celebrate your youth because you'll be older for much longer than you'll be young. Make the most of each day and have fun. Prepare for your future, but don't obsess over it. Everything that's supposed to happen will happen when it's supposed to happen. So lighten up.

Here are some ways that you can enjoy being a teen.

- Rent a funny movie and invite a few friends to come over and watch it over popcorn and pizza.

- Have a water balloon fight on a hot summer's day with a few friends.

- Pull a harmless prank on your parents, then let them in on the joke.

- Join the youth group in your church, school, or community center or start one.

What are some other things that you can do to enjoy being a teen?

_____
_____
_____
_____
_____
_____
_____
_____
_____
_____
_____
_____
_____
_____
_____
_____
_____
_____
_____
_____
_____
_____

Power Move #50
Pass It On

There's an expression that goes, "The more you know, the more you grow." And the more you grow the more you owe. What this means is the more you learn, the more you need to be sharing your knowledge with others. In essence, you need to pass it on. The fact that you've gotten this far in the book means that you now have forty-nine power moves that will enable you to prepare yourself for success. You can begin to pass it on by sharing some of the strategies in this book with your friends, classmates, parents, and teachers. Talk to them about which power moves you like best and why. Talk to them about simple ways that they can start making power moves in their own lives.

Many teens often feel like they have nothing to contribute, but this is not true. You can contribute to humanity by sharing your knowledge, experience and insight with others. Don't underestimate your ability to effect change. Even if you were on the wrong track in the past, you can still help others by educating them about the dangers of engaging in destructive behavior.

Think about the people you respect the most. They can be people you know personally or people you've never met whom you greatly admire. How do they pass it on? How do they share their knowledge with others? Do they keep their experiences to themselves or do they make a conscious effort to school others? I'll bet that they share their knowledge with others. And when they do, they become a tremendous source of wisdom and inspiration for others.

Create a list of ways that you can pass it on.

_____

_____

_____

Power Move #51
Don't Just Speak About It, Be About It

It's not enough to talk the talk, you've got to walk the walk. Success doesn't happen for those who simply talk about it, it happens for those who put in the effort to make it happen. You can be and do anything you want as long as you are willing to put in the time and effort. You can make it, but no one is going to put in the effort for you. That's your responsibility.

For some people, success is spelled $UCCE$$, because they equate success with money and material possessions. But that's only a small part of success. There are plenty of people who have lots of money, but are miserable. So money does not equal success. True success is living a happy and a healthy life as you pursue your dreams. It's not so much about what you do for a living, what kind of car you drive, how much money you make or how nice your clothes are, it's really about who you are as a person and how you live each day of your life. Success doesn't come to you; you make it happen each day by the choices you make.

How do you begin to walk the path of success? You can begin the journey towards success by adopting these simple habits:

1) Encourage yourself daily by reading something inspirational, saying a positive affirmation, surrounding yourself with positive people and participating in any positive activity that boosts your self-esteem.

2) Set high standards for yourself and always put your best foot forward.

3) Set goals and work towards achieving them one small step at a time.

4) Take responsibility for your actions, your future, your life.

5) Stay away from negative people and negative situations.

6) Make education a priority and learn something new each day.

7) Turn obstacles into opportunities for growth.

8) Help and share with others.

9) Reach out for support. Get connected to other teens and adults who can help you achieve your goals.

10) Keep the faith. Remember that divine order is working things out on your behalf.

As mentioned throughout this book, success doesn't come to you; you make it happen each day by choosing to be responsible and productive. You make it happen, by getting your education, learning the skills that you need to learn in order to go far in life and by staying away from negativity. You decide how successful you become by making smart choices and pursuing your goals.

If you really want to make it, you've got to take your success seriously and strive for excellence every day of your life. It sounds like a lot of work and it is, but in the long run it's worth it. If you make the daily commitment to choose success over mediocrity, you will be able to create a life you'll love. Go for it.

Power Move #52
Keep On Keeping On

When everything goes wrong,
And you feel like you can't go on,
Juts hold your head high and keep on keeping on;
When challenges come you way,
And your plans all go astray,
Sit back, be still and pray and keep on keeping on;
When people put you down,
And toss your name around,
Don't sweat it, don't regret it – just keep on keeping on;
If you persevere and stick it out,
Push past fear and move through doubt,
You will win because you kept on keeping on.
Cassandra Mack

To keep on keeping on means to keep moving forward no matter what obstacles come your way. It's about pushing yourself a little harder and a little further so that you can accomplish all that you set out to do. All successful people have three things in common. They all keep moving forward despite the challenges they face. They strive for excellence, not perfection. And they look at every failure and challenging situation as an opportunity to learn and grow.

There is nothing in life that you cannot do, no goal that you cannot achieve and no obstacle that you cannot overcome, if you keep moving forward. It's all up to you, because you are the most important ingredient in your success. All you have to do is believe it. You have inner strength on your side, potential that you are just beginning to tap and natural strengths that will keep getting stronger. You also have God watching over you. With this in mind you are unstoppable!

CLOSING WORDS

It is my hope that the 52 power moves help you to take positive charge of your life and rise above the challenges that you may face. Never, ever give up because everything you want is within your reach.

Go make it happen! I'm cheering for you.

Young, Gifted and Doing It

Success Action Planner

Stop, Look and Take Action

Think about your life as it is now and where you would like it to be going. Think about the attitudes and behaviors you need to change in order to get where you'd like to go. Write down the attitudes and behaviors that are holding you back and what you need to do to change them. Keep this list handy to remind yourself what you need to work on in order to grow.

_____
_____
_____
_____
_____
_____
_____
_____

Now that you've identified the attitudes and behaviors that are holding you back, you need to think about the type of person you want to become. Envision the type of person you want to become and write it in the space below. Keep it handy in order to check it on a regular basis to see how much closer you are to becoming your best self.

_____
_____
_____
_____
_____
_____
_____

Going for Your Goals

To get an idea of what you really want in life, go through the list that I've provided and rate each goal in descending order from most important to least important. The goals that you rate as the top three are probably most important to you. When you are finished with the list that I have provided, add a couple of your own goals.

_____ to improve my math skills.

_____ to improve my reading comprehension and writing skills.

_____ to improve my school attendance.

_____ to find a part-time or weekend job.

_____ to start my own part-time business.

_____ to improve my relationships with others.

_____ to gain experience by volunteering or interning.

_____ to graduate from high school and go on to college.

_____ to get my GED and go to college.

_____ to improve my spending habits.

_____ to learn new skills.

_____ to take better care of my health.

_____ to build up my confidence and self-esteem.

To _____

To _____

To _____

Sometimes when we set out to achieve our goals we will be faced with obstacles and challenges. If you are able to identify possible obstacles, then you're one step ahead of the game. Think about all the things you want to achieve, accomplish and contribute and write down the possible obstacles. After you've identified the possible obstacles write down how you intend to overcome them.

This is how I intend to overcome the obstacles that stand in my way: _____

_____

Strengths and Weaknesses

In order to go far in life, you need to know what your strengths and weaknesses are. We all have strengths and weaknesses. The more accurately you're able to identify yours, the easier it will be to go after what you want. Why? Because you'll be able to build on your strengths and work on your weaknesses.

My Strengths

My Weaknesses

Now that you've identified your strengths and weaknesses, make a promise to yourself to work on your weaknesses. Start with one and work on the others one week at a time. Check in with yourself to see how well you're doing.

Talk to Other People

When you talk to people about your dreams, plans and goals, you begin to create a network of positive people who can support you on your journey. And the clearer you are about what you're trying to do, you'll find that people will go out of their way to help you. So start talking to other people. Create a list below of the people you need to talk to in order to expand your network.

Person's Name	Telephone Number/ Email

Your Self-Check List

Throughout this book I have stressed the importance of believing in yourself and having a positive attitude. What determines how far you go in life more than anything else is your attitude. The attitude that you have about yourself can make you or it can break you. Use this self-check list to get more in tune with how you feel about yourself.

My attitude towards myself is:

_____

_____

_____

My attitude towards life is:

_____

_____

_____

My behavior towards myself reflects that I:

_____

_____

_____

My behavior towards others reflects that I:

_____

_____

_____

I care for myself by:

_____

_____

I show myself that I love myself by:

_____

_____

_____

My hygiene and grooming habits tell others that I:

_____

_____

_____

To motivate myself I usually:

_____

_____

_____

My grades reflect that I:

_____

_____

_____

The people I hang out with reflect that I:

_____

_____

_____

Get to Work

What steps are you willing to take to prepare yourself for success? Write down the steps that you will take to position yourself for success.

Today I will:

_____

_____

_____

Tomorrow I will:

_____

_____

_____

By next week I will:

_____

_____

_____

By next month I will:

_____

_____

_____

By this time next year I will:

_____

_____

_____

Tips for Parents, Teachers and Youth Service Providers

Helping teens grow into their potential and take positive charge of their lives takes time, effort and compassion. But if we do not put in the work, we will have to work twice as hard to undo the consequences of unrealized potential, limited life skills and social unpreparedness. Following are ten tips that identify actions that parents, teachers and youth service providers can take to build assets in youth.

1. Help Them To Believe In Themselves

If a teen believes in himself, he will see himself as valuable, competent, lovable and worthy. He will have a positive sense of self and a healthy self-image. He will be confident in himself as a person and in his capabilities. Teens with high self-esteem will be optimistic about their futures and will believe in their ability to accomplish their goals.

It will be difficult for a teen to believe in herself if her parents, teachers and other significant adults in her life do not show her that she's competent, accepted for who she is and that she matters. Show them that you value their uniqueness and individuality. Let them know what you admire and respect about them. Make a conscious effort to notice their strengths and draw out their talents. Give them special tasks so that they can begin to see themselves as capable and valuable.

2. Accept Them for Who They Are

Every teen needs to be accepted for who they are, even if they occasionally make choices that you don't agree with. If a teen feels like your love, commitment and emotional support are based on whether or not he can live up to your standards, then he will never feel worthy enough to gain your acceptance or emotionally safe enough to let down his guard.

While you don't want to ignore troubling behavior, you also don't want to devastate them with destructive criticism either. Try not to lose faith in a teen when she makes a bad decision.

Instead of pointing out how disappointed you are in her as a person, focus your disapproval on her behavior. You can say something like: *I find it very disrespectful when you ... Or, right now I'm annoyed with you because ...* Depersonalizing your response enables a teen to take in what you are saying and understand the main point of your comments.

3. Be Part of Their Support System

Every teen needs someone in their life who they can go to when they need encouragement, advice or refuge. Every teen needs someone who will help them through a tough time and point them in the right direction when they need it. It may not take much more than a kind word, listening with undivided attention or providing them with resources so they can get the help that they need.

Have periodic discussions with teens about the importance of putting a support system in place. Encourage teens to find mentors and join after-school and weekend programs. Be on the look out for signs of stress and depression in teens. Have names and numbers of community resources readily available.

4. Have High Expectations

Expect your teens to succeed. Talk about success. Share your successes and the obstacles that you had to overcome to get where you are today. Celebrate their achievements both big and small. Help teens to stretch themselves and reach higher. Help teens to understand that failure goes hand in hand with success. Encourage teens to turn setbacks into opportunities and to rise above adverse circumstances.

5. Don't Underestimate the Power of Peer Pressure

During adolescence peer pressure is at an all time high. A teen's need to declare his independence coupled with the desire to fit in with peers makes him more susceptible to peer pressure. The best way to help teens resist negative peer pressure is to help them build a healthy sense of self, gain clarity about their values and discuss potential risky situations that they might encounter along with strategies for avoiding them. Discuss the issue of peer pressure with your son, daughter or youth group and ask for ideas and strategies that teenagers can use to avoid giving in to negative peer pressure.

6. Broaden Their Sense of Achievement

Every teen has a range of skills, strengths and talents. Some may be good at sports, surviving in the wilderness and carpentry. While others might be good at drawing, styling hair, managing their time or writing poetry or prose. Teens can really thrive when they are made aware of the many strengths and talents they posses. Every teen will benefit from believing that he can be successful at something and that down the road he can turn that skill or talent into a paying career.

As adults who care about youth, one of our roles is to identify and build on the strengths that youth posses. Academic achievement should never be the only measure of a teen's intelligence.

7. Stress the Importance of Reading

I believe that there's nothing that can expand one's horizons like reading. Except, maybe traveling. Read and learn with your son, daughter or youth group. Share books that inspired you or helped you to explore the endless possibilities. Start a reading group. Make it fun and interesting. If you don't have a library card, go out and get one. Better yet, make it a family outing or class trip. Stress the importance of learning for the sake of learning. Show teens how they can apply the information they learn from the books that they read in their day-to-day lives.

8. Promote Responsibility and Self-Management

Encouraging responsibility and self-management helps teens develop their decision-making skills, organizational skills and it builds their self-esteem. Be adamant about promoting the use of personal organizers, calendars and day planners. Let teens share in decision making by asking for their input and ideas. Take their ideas under serious consideration. Show your teens that it's ok to have views that differ from yours. This enables them to stand firm in their decisions when they have to take an unpopular stance or go against the crowd. Teach your teens to make good decisions so that you can learn to trust their judgment. Whenever possible, respect their choices.

9. Model What You Expect

One of the most powerful things that you can do for your son, daughter or youth group is to model the type of behavior you expect from your teens. Lead by example. This reinforces appropriate boundaries and expectations, demonstrates positive values and it makes you a more consistent parent, teacher or youth service provider. When teens see the adults in their lives living by the ideals that they teach, it strengthens their respect for you and boosts your credibility.

Our values and beliefs are conveyed by the things we say as well as the things we do. So it should come as no surprise that teens look to us to set the example. Be diligent about setting a positive example.

10. Never Give Up

It goes without saying that this is one of the most important tips. Never give up on your teens. Keep believing in them. Keep guiding them. Keep pushing them to aim higher.

Discussion Guide for Parents, Teachers and Youth Service Providers

The discussion questions in this section are designed to stimulate thinking, spark conversations and encourage more dialogue between adults and teenagers. Before using the discussion guide, read the book thoroughly. Reflect on the issues presented. Then, get together with a group of parents and their teens or your youth group and initiate a discussion around the questions in this guide.

1. In Power Move #1. *Become the Director and Producer of Your Life*, the author says that we all have the ability to decide whether our lives will be a hit or a miss. Do you believe that teens have the ability to determine whether or not they will lead happy and successful lives? Why or why not? Do you believe that everyone has the potential to be happy and successful? What does success mean to you? Do you believe you're on the road to success? What does happiness mean to you? Are you happy? Can you think of three people who seem happy and successful? What makes them a success in your eyes? What can adults do to help teens position themselves for success?

2. In Power Move #3. *Believe In Yourself*, the author says that whatever we believe about ourselves becomes true for us because we usually act in accordance to our beliefs. Do you agree with this statement? Why or why not? What are the consequences of not believing in yourself? Have you ever known anyone who had great potential but never did anything with it because they didn't believe in themselves? What does self-confidence mean to you and how do we get it? How does one's self-confidence affect their academic performance, friendships and romantic relationships? What can adults do to help teens build their confidence?

3. Is it important to have goals? Why or why not? How can you tell if a person has goals? Can a person live their dreams and accomplish a lot in life if they do not have any goals? In Power Move #8. *Set S.M.A.R.T. Goals,* the author says that goals are important because they help you to plan a course of action and give you a sense of purpose. Besides the two things that the author just mentioned, what else can goals help you with?

4. In Power Move #11. *Don't Let The Past Keep You From Moving Forward,* the author stresses the importance of making peace with your past and not allowing unresolved anger to get the best of you. Do you think it's easy or difficult to let go of the past? How can staying stuck in the past prevent you from moving forward? Besides talking to an adult you trust what else can teens do to move forward if they've had a difficult past?

5. Do friends and classmates ever hate on each other? Why do you think that some people hate on each other? Have you ever hated on someone else? Explain. Have you ever been hated on? Explain. In Power Move #5. *Don't Hate, Congratulate,* the author says that it doesn't make sense to be jealous of or compare yourself to other people because the only comparison that really counts is the one you make against your own potential. Do you think this is easier said than done? Why or why not? What are some things that people can do to keep envy and jealousy in check?

6. Some teens give into the pressure to smoke cigarettes, drink alcohol and do drugs, while others do not. Why do you think some teens have more difficulty staying away from cigarettes, alcohol and drugs? In Power Move #14. *Keep A Clear Head,* the author says that most people who use drugs think that they can handle it and that they won't develop an addiction. Do you know anyone who feels this way? Do you think that they are handling things well? What are the dangers of smoking, drinking and doing drugs? Is there a great deal of pressure for teens your age

to smoke, drink and use drugs? What can teens do to resist the temptation to smoke, drink and get high?

7. In Power Move #15. *Keep It On Lock,* the author urges teens to hold off on sex. Is there a great deal of pressure for teens your age to have sex? What is the age of the youngest person you know having sex? What are some of the risks of having sex? Do guys and girls view sex differently? Can two people express affection without having any kind of sexual contact? How far is too far when it comes to expressing affection? Is it considered cool or corny to abstain from sex? What are the benefits of holding off on sex?

8. In Power Move #31. *Don't Let Fear Hold You Back,* the author says that in many instances fear is the only thing that stands in the way of a person's ability to achieve his or her goals. Have you ever been in a situation where you were afraid to try something new only to be pleasantly surprised by how much you enjoyed yourself or how well you did? Do you know anyone who has allowed fear to hold them back from going after their dreams or trying something new? What is the cost of allowing fear to hold you back?

9. In Power Move #35. *Keep Your Parents In the Mix,* the author encourages teens to talk to their parents about the important stuff. Is it easy or difficult for teens to talk to their parents? What issues are easy to talk about? What issues are difficult? Are there any benefits to keeping your parents in the mix? What can parents do to get their teens to open up to them more?

10. In Power Move #36. *Accentuate the Positive,* the author stresses the importance of figuring out your likes, dislikes, strengths and weaknesses in order to put your best foot forward. Besides these tips what else can teens do to accentuate the positive?

11. In Power Move #44. *Learn Something New Each Day*, the author encourages teens to learn one new word each day and read five pages above your required reading. Do you think this power move can benefit you? Why or why not? What subjects do you like most? What subjects are your least favorite? What book have you read this year that inspired you or that you really enjoyed? What book would you recommend that every teenager read?

12. Throughout the book, the author's underlying themes are: believe in yourself, take responsibility for your life and keep on keeping on. What else can teens do to walk the path of success?

9 Keys for Leading A Successful Young, Gifted and Doing It Group

If you are a group leader, counselor, educator, social worker or other caring adult looking to start your own leadership, life skills or success group for teens, you can use the information in this book as a springboard to generate ideas and session topics. Teaching teenagers to develop the mindset and habits that lead to lifelong success is very empowering. It helps to limit high-risk behavior, it builds assets and enables teens to develop the mental, emotional and social skills that will put them on the pathway to excellence. Here are nine keys for leading a successful, *Young, Gifted and Doing It* group.

1. Think About Your Overall Purpose for Wanting To Offer This Group and Set Clear Goals To Help You Measure The Group's Progress

It is important that both you and your teens understand why you are offering this group. What will they get out of the group? What will they learn? How will they benefit? What are your goals and objectives?

2. Select A Regular Meeting Location and Time

Where will you meet? Try to find a meeting space that is welcoming, comfortable and spacious enough to accommodate interactive activities. How often will you meet? Once a week? Bi-weekly? Once a month? How long will each session last? One hour? Ninety-minutes? Two hours? How long will the group run? One year? Six months? Three months? You need to find a meeting location and identify a regular start time and end time. This builds consistency and continuity.

3. Set Clear Expectations and Limits

For your group to run smoothly you need to establish some basic ground rules around: time, attendance, conduct within the group and what stays confidential and what does not. Make sure these rules are posted and distributed.

4. Team Up With Another Group Leader

A team of two facilitators is best. It allows for different strengths and leadership styles. It enables the group to continue if one of the leaders need to be absent for one reason or another. It models the skill of teamwork.

5. Educate Yourself On How To Facilitate Teen Groups

Attend workshops. Read books on facilitating groups for teenagers. Make a commitment to provide high quality leadership by building your skills and knowledge in the areas of adolescent development and group facilitation.

6. Make the Group Interactive

Allow conversations to flow freely among the teens once you've introduced a topic or asked a question. You role as a facilitator is to listen more than you speak and to make sure that everyone is heard and that everyone feels safe. This encourages the teens to make the group their own. Also, look for fun and interesting activities that build on the session topics. Build these activities into each session.

7. Get Buy-in From Parents and Other Key Stakeholders

If you are a youth service provider, thinking about running a *Young, Gifted and Doing It Group* out of your agency, get buy in from parents and other key stakeholders. Keep parents informed of the group's progress. Have a special power move meeting for parents. Identify other stakeholders and include them in the planning and recruitment process. Perhaps they can assist you with finding resources or guest speakers for your group.

If you are a parent, get buy-in from other parents in your neighborhood. Allow them to help you. Perhaps there are parents in your community who have access to resources or information that can benefit the group.

8. Familiarize Yourself With Community Resources

Find out what services and programs are available in your community. Create a resource listing of helpful telephone numbers and websites like: libraries, recreational and sports programs, mentoring programs, cultural arts, tutorial services and mental well ness programs. Have this list readily available for teens and their parents.

9. Remember It's Their Group

Teenagers have valuable information to share. Ask them for their ideas and input. Then, implement them. Let them lead a power move session or two. Show them that you respect their ideas and opinions.

Resources for Teens

Community Service
If you want to make a difference in your community contact:
> ➤ America's Charities
>   1-800-458-9505
> ➤ Youth Service America
>   1-202-296-2992
> ➤ Center for Community Service
>   www.jcu.edu/comserv
> ➤ YMCA
>   1-800-333-4622

Drug and Alcohol Prevention/ Intervention
If you or someone you care about is using drugs or drinking contact:
> ➤ Al-Anon/Al teen
>   1-800-356-9996
> ➤ Drug and Alcohol treatment network
>   www.drugnet.net

Educational Alternatives
To find out about alternative educational programs contact:
> ➤ School-to-Work
>   1-800-251-7236
> ➤ Youth Build
>   1-617-623-9900

Job Training and Information
For job training and information contact:
> ➤ America's One Stop Career Center System
>   1-212-337-2139
> ➤ Center for Employment and Training
>   1-800-533-2519
> ➤ STRIVE
>   1-212-360-1100
> ➤ Job corps website
>   www.jobcorps.org

Mentoring
To be a mentor or find one contact:
- ➢ Big Brothers Big Sisters of America
1-215-567-7000
- ➢ National Mentoring Partnership
1-202-338-3844

STD's
If you or someone you care about needs information on how to protect yourself against sexually transmitted diseases contact:
- ➢ Sexually Transmitted Diseases
1-800-227-8922
- ➢ STD Prevention
www.stdprevention.com
- ➢ Youth only AIDS line
1-800-788-1234

Sexual Assault/Incest
If you or someone you know is the victim of sexual assault, incest or rape contact:
- ➢ National Abuse Hotline
1-800-422-4453
- ➢ Sex Abuse Hotline
1-800-656-4673
- ➢ Foothills rape crisis center
1-800-585-8952

Therapy/Counseling
If you are going through a difficult problem or just need someone to help you sort things out contact:
- ➢ Covenant House Nine-Line
1-800-999-9999
- ➢ National Institute of Mental Health
1-800-64-PANIC
- ➢ National Youth Crisis Hotline
1-800-448-4663

Send In Your . . .
Young, Gifted and Doing It Success Story!

Success stories for and by teens are a powerful source of inspiration and hope. Your success story can provide other teens with the motivation and encouragement that they need to take charge of their lives and overcome difficult challenges.

After you have begun to apply the power moves presented in this book and you've had some success in either achieving one of your goals or overcoming a very challenging situation, share your success story with me by e-mailing me at: teenpowermove@aol.com.

I'd love to hear about how this book has impacted your life.

Cassandra Mack

About the Author

Cassandra Mack, M.S.W. is a national workshop presenter and consultant on youth development issues. Cassandra's workshops for professionals who work with youth and parents raising teens include: *"Empowering Girls for Life,"* *"Helping Teens Build Self-esteem from Head to Toe."* Her keynotes for teens include: *"Don't Believe the Hype: Success is in Your Hands,"* and *"Elevating Your Game."*

Over the years, Cassandra has appeared on Good Day New York, Voices from the Village and What Woman Want. She has written articles for The New York Beacon, BELLE, Guidelines and Black Love. She's been profiled in the Network Journal and has spoken at numerous youth service organizations, schools, community organizations, women's groups and churches.

In addition to *Young, Gifted and Doing It,* Cassandra has written three other books. They are: *Smart Moves That Successful Youth Workers Make* and *Her Rite of Passage: How to Design and Deliver A Rites of Passage Program for African-American Girls and Young Women,* and *Cool, Confident and Strong: 52 Power Moves for Girls.*

Cassandra was born and raised in New York and has taken her powerful message of success and empowerment to youth and youth service professionals across the country. Cassandra received her Bachelor's degree in Speech from Brooklyn College and her Master's degree in Social Work from Hunter College.

For more information on Cassandra Mack's workshops and motivational programs visit her online at: ***www.empoweredliving.net***

To book Cassandra to address your teens or staff or to contact her about putting together a staff or youth leadership retreat for your organization:

E-mail her at: empoweredliving4u@yahoo.com

Visit her on the web at: www.strategiesforempoweredliving.com

Other Books By The Author

Cool, Confident and Strong: 52 Power Moves for Girls. ($12.95). This book provides pre-teen and teenage girls with the tools they need to take decisions that respect their values and boundaries.

Smart Moves That Successful Youth Workers Make. ($24.95)
In this book you'll learn: the 7 roles of the front-line youth worker, how to avoid the 10 biggest mistakes smart youth workers make and how to build assets in youth.

Young, Gifted and Doing It: 52 Power Moves for Teens. ($14.95)
From resisting peer pressure to setting goals and making education a top priority, this book is the definitive success guide for teens.

- To purchase any of these products go to:
  www.strategiesforempoweredliving.com

978-0-595-46789-1
0-595-46789-X

Made in the USA
Lexington, KY
10 August 2015